SEARCHING
FOR SHALOM

Books by Ann Weems
Published by Westminster/John Knox Press

Family Faith Stories

Reaching for Rainbows
  Resources for Creative Worship

Kneeling in Bethlehem

SEARCHING FOR SHALOM

Resources for Creative Worship

ANN WEEMS

Westminster/John Knox Press
Louisville, Kentucky

Scripture quotations from the Revised Standard Version of the Bible are copyright 1946, 1952, © 1971, 1973 by the Division of Christian Education of the National Council of the Churches of Christ in the U.S.A. and are used by permission.

Book design by Ken Taylor

First edition

Published by Westminster/John Knox Press
Louisville, Kentucky

PRINTED IN THE UNITED STATES OF AMERICA
9   8   7   6   5   4   3

Library of Congress Cataloging-in-Publication Data

Weems, Ann, 1934–
    Searching for shalom : resources for creative worship / by Ann Weems. — 1st ed.
        p.   cm.
    ISBN 0-664-25223-0

    1. Worship programs.   2. Peace—Religious aspects—
Christianity.
I. Title.
BV198.W384 1991
264'.13—dc20   91-11975

To Dan Ross, my teacher and my friend,
in joyful gratitude for every star you flung my way—

SEARCHING
FOR SHALOM

CONTENTS

9

THE HOLY IN THE ORDINARY

WOMEN OF FAITH

SERVICES OF WORSHIP

ACKNOWLEDGMENTS

The author offers grateful acknowledgment to the following publishers for permission to reprint the poems listed below.

To the Mission Interpretation and Promotion office of the Stewardship and Communication Development Ministry Unit, Presbyterian Church (U.S.A.): for "Prayer of Confession," "Litany of Confession," "Prayer of Confession" (retitled "Forgive Us"), "Prayer of Thanksgiving," "Prayer of Stewardship," "Our Gifts Are Gifts of Hope," "Our Lord Is Called Hope," "The Widow's Mite," "Jesus Encounters Zacchaeus," "Casting Out the Moneychangers," "The Parable of the Talents," "The Rich Young Ruler," and " 'Where Your Treasure Is . . . ,' " from *Abound in Hope*.

To The Westminster Press, for "All of Us Good Church People Know the Story," "It Was Faith That Made Noah Go Into the Unknown," and "Sarah, You Are Not the Only One," from *Family Faith Stories* (copyright © 1985 Ann Weems); for "Into This Silent Night," from *Kneeling in Bethlehem* (© 1980, 1985, 1987 Ann Weems); and for "Are We Clapping for the Wrong God?" from *Reaching for Rainbows: Resources for Creative Worship* (copyright © 1980 The Westminster Press).

To *Presbyterian Survey*, for material first printed in "Advent Calendar 1987."

Material quoted in "Sojourner Truth, the Spirit of Change" is excerpted from *Narrative of Sojourner Truth* and

PREFACE

In recent years, congregations have seen an increasing emphasis on the biblical theme of "shalom." References to shalom are cropping up in our Bible classes and appearing in curriculum and other printed material used in efforts toward "peacemaking," as well as in theological books written for both clergy and laity. It is also emerging with greater frequency in liturgy and sermons. We used to sign our letters, "Peace!"; now we sign them, "Shalom!", and with increasing regularity we greet each other with this strange and wonder-filled blessing.

I say "strange and wonder-filled" because the more I study and learn about our shalom story, the less I seem to understand just exactly what it is we're saying to one another with this greeting, this hope. Are you wishing me prosperity? Are you wishing me wealth? Are you wishing me land? Are you wishing me a lifetime in the wilderness with the hope that I'll get to the Promised Land? Are you wishing me a peaceful existence? Are you wishing me a world with no war? Are you wishing me a life of faithfulness in spite of the risk such a life involves? On and on and on . . .

The word "shalom" is not easily defined—certainly not in one word (peace) and certainly not in the negative (the absence of war). The roots of the meaning of shalom are deep and entangled and, rather like the roots of a large and ancient tree, roam in places that are not easily seen. To dig the roots up is an overwhelming task. I'll leave the digging to the biblical scholars; I've been scratching, and I've been searching—for shalom. What I've found is this: Shalom is much more than my own personal prosperity. It's much more than land for me and for my family. It's much more than a sense of well-being. It's much more than quiet and calmness, much more than the absence of stress. It's much more than the "peace" you and I wish each other, much more than no war, no conflict, no violence, no arguing, no loud voices and no red faces. It certainly *is* a peace that passes my own understanding. Shalom is something that won't come from wishing on a star or keeping the rules. It's nothing I can buy with wealth or power or prestige. It's a gift, a gift that was promised. It's something I keep searching for and hoping for, but something I know I can't have if you don't have it, you and all the yous out there in this world. This book is about searching, searching for shalom—my searching, your searching, our searching together in this community that we call the church of Jesus Christ. My hope is that we can be the "Shalom Church" and the "Shalom Persons" that Walter Brueggemann writes of in his book *Living Toward a Vision*—a church community willing to risk the wilderness because we believe in the word of God.

On an Indian summer day last fall, I visited Dan and Dorothy Ross on their family farm in Clarksville, Tennessee. I was greeted with the same enthusiastic welcome I got every time I went to their home in Memphis, where Dan taught at Southwestern, a Presbyterian college (now Rhodes College). Dorothy, an art historian as well as an artist, exudes her artistry in everything she does. The house is filled with works of art they have collected from travels, from artist friends, from students, and from Dorothy's creativity (and Dan's). Even our luncheon was a work of art. She had gone to a great deal of trouble. I felt celebrated! Dan, retired professor, writer, now farmer, read to me (at my request) from his recently published work. We talked about ourselves, our families, our current lives. We talked about the state of the world and about writing and writers and art and politics and faith and worship and causes they were engaged in, causes of justice and of mercy (although they didn't say that); and Dan told stories as he used to do in class, and we talked about darkness, and we talked about hope, and we laughed a lot . . . especially at Dan's gentle swats at society's and the church's sacred cows. I could have stayed there much longer, feasting my eyes on the art, listening to the music and the reading, engaging in warm conversation with these two very remarkable people, soaking up the love of life they both exude, each in a different but compelling way. As I said good-bye and drove on, I realized that they live in grateful celebration, with humor and with humility and with tears for the world's darkness. They live searching for shalom with a familiarity that comes from daily searching. That makes for abundant living. I drove on, but I took with me the blessing of having been with these two "shalom persons."

The well-being, the blessedness, and the peace that we all want for ourselves and for the world will not come with new programs or new organization—not even with a new minister! If we continue our searching, and at least think about leaving our security for the wilderness in an effort to live toward the promised land (see Brueggemann, *Living Toward the Vision,* chapter 14), perhaps we will find new hearts and new vision to live our faith, knowing that the promise has been kept, that the Promised One was sent to live among us, that shalom is ours if we have the eyes to see.

SEARCHING
FOR
SHALOM

SEARCHING FOR SHALOM

I keep searching for shalom,
    drawing my water from one well after another—
    but still I thirst
for the shower of blessing
    that is shalom.

I yearn
    for life to be just and merciful and peaceful,
    but the streets are filled with daily deaths
of spirit and of flesh
    . . . but no shalom.

I keep searching for shalom,
    away from crowds and commotion,
    but peace and quiet
don't blot the pain
    of broken hearts and broken bodies.

I keep searching for shalom,
    thinking perhaps I'll find it
    in a quiet field of flowers
or in star or sea or snow,
    but still the innocent are trampled.

I keep searching for shalom,
    standing in holy places,

sitting among saints.
Surely in the sanctuary
    I will find shalom.

I keep searching for shalom,
    but holy places
    are not magic.
Good works and printed prayers
    don't guarantee shalom.

Beyond cathedral walls
    and above ethereal music,
    the blaring din of death persists.
Back in the streets,
    the people walk in darkness.

I keep searching for shalom.
    I have pursued
    and sought it.
Have I looked in all
    the wrong places?

What is this bonding,
    this glue among us,
    this cohesiveness
that holds us in the hope
    of shalom?

The longing won't die.
    The hope keeps emerging
    like a new sprout
that perseveres on the stump
    of a felled tree.

Even in the daily barrage
    of obscenities
    some new star melts
into my eyes
    and the promise persists.

Here in the darkness
   some new light
   stirs within me.
Here in the streets
   I find shalom.

Shalom lives
   not in the sanctuary,
   but in the streets . . .
in chaos
   on a cross.

In the face of Jesus
   is the peace
   that passes all understanding
the everlasting Sabbath . . .
   Shalom!

HOPE GROWING IN WINTER

I was surprised
  in January
by a crocus growing
  right outside my kitchen door:
a splotch of spring
  that burst through winter's veil.

Surprised again—
  in just two weeks
I couldn't find
  the crocus for the snow,
fresh fallen,
  the last laughter in winter's fling.

It is buried now,
  my crocus;
hidden, but not forgotten,
  for I know it's there . . .
hope growing in winter,
  shalom beneath the snow.

I SEE YOUR PAIN

I see your pain
  and want to banish it
    with the wave of a star,
but have no star.

I see your tears
  and want to dry them
    with the hem of an angel's gown,
but have no angel.

I see your heart fallen to the ground
  · and want to return it
    wrapped in cloths woven of rainbow,
but have no rainbow.

God is the One
  who has stars, and angels and rainbows,
and I am the one
  God sends to sit beside you
    until the stars come out
      and the angels dry your tears
        and your heart is back in place,
          rainbow blessed.

FAMILY

Our conversation is spent in talking
    too much about the domestic,
    too little in speaking our hearts—
    too much about finances,
    too little about the value of love—
    too much about catching cobwebs,
    too little about dust-covered dreams—
    too much about laundry,
    too little about cleaning temples within—
    too much about going for groceries,
    too little about food for our souls—
    too much about earthly possessions,
    too little about storing treasures in heaven—
    too much chastising,
    too little cherishing—
    too much blame,
    too few balloons—
Before it's too late,
    let's speak of feelings that have been hidden
      behind bank payments and orthodontic visits and
        the PTA.
Before the music stops,
    let's speak our hearts
      and laugh a star or two.

IN THE NIGHT

In the night
   when our world dissolves in tears
we feel
                  abandoned.

   Nobody knows
      and nobody understands
         and nobody feels
            our pain.
   Even the ones who care
      don't care
         the way
            we do.

In that moment
   when there is no sound
      and there is no sight,
nothing but the silent unrelenting night . . .
   in that moment
      comes the choice
         of Death or Life:
We can look down into our own Self
   or we can look up to God,
         the only Star in our unlit skies.

FORGIVENESS

I was wrong,
   arrogantly
      self-righteously
wrong.
   So interested in being understood,
      I didn't understand.
   So anxious to be right,
      I didn't see your pain.
How is it then
   that you're the one
      to bring the flowers?

AN APRIL PLACE

I used to wish an April place
   for you and me to go
a private place
a special place
   where no one else would know
but then one day it came to me
   when looking at your face
that anywhere when I'm with you
   becomes an April place.

GOD

God is the Question with whom we contend
    throughout our lives.
God is the One standing there
    in the closing of doors and the opening of windows.
God is the Surprising Voice that calls
    in the jaggedness of life.
God is the Hand that keeps the world
    from snuffing out the stars.
God is the Poem that begins and ends
    in a circle.
God is the Circle
    that neither begins nor ends.

MORNING STAR

There are those times when
   all the stars are torn from our skies,
   and morning will not come.
We try to make our way
   in unlit passages,
   frightened, desperate and despairing.
We cannot see,
   for wherever we turn
   the night continues,
And yet, it is
   into this impenetrable night
   that the Child is born.
Tearing through the seams of darkness,
   the Morning Star appears
   in our eyes and in our hearts.
The people who walked in darkness
   have seen
   a great Light.

JOSHUA'S RAINBOW

Joshua's rainbow hugs his house,
   arching snugly over roof and down again.
Adjacent sunflowers, orange and yellow, loom large,
   as tall as the rainbow.
Somehow the house smiles,
   or perhaps it's Joshua
      smiling through the paint.

I hold his creation in my hand,
   this paper found upon my doorstep,
and conjure images of this child
   suddenly and tearfully aware of his loss,
or his disappointed mother
   searching sidewalks with a flashlight,
      deep into the night.

Perhaps Joshua just tired of the game:
   one more picture to carry home,
one more picture to go from hand
   to refrigerator to a drawer somewhere.
Of course, he might have dropped it,
   simply or deliberately dropped it,
      weary of the routine.

Or maybe other children ridiculed his efforts—
   making fun of the rainbow hugging his house,

and the too-large sunflowers,
   orange and yellow . . .
so that Joshua, embarrassed and temporarily defeated,
   threw down the drawing
      in a gesture of not caring.

I suppose it'd be too much to hope that
   Joshua saw the rainbow above our door,
and felt a kindred spirit,
   and even entertained the thought
that perhaps someone who lived here
   would understand and appreciate
      his perception.

Whatever happened, the artist
   —as a very young man—
created his inward smile
   upon manila paper,
and somehow his creation
   found its way into the heart of another
      who celebrates hugging rainbows,
         smiling houses,
            and overzealous sunflowers.

Who knows through what mysterious notes of grace
   our inner smiling spirits
      connect . . .
I do know
I am smiling now
   and so is my spirit.
Thank you, God . . . for Joshua.

THE GIFT

We had everything she did not have,
   and so we gave to her our singing
      at Christmastime.
Young and healthy, we came from homes
   with trees and lights she'd never see
      and gifts she'd never open.
Bedridden, she greeted us with clapping hands
   and a smile that never left
      her wrinkled face.
We caroled and caroled in that tiny room,
   and she closed her eyes in ecstasy
      and even sang along
         from time to time.
As we were leaving,
   she thanked us all profusely
      and passed to me
         her "offering."
I looked in my hand
   and saw a crumpled dollar bill
      and looked into her eyes
         and saw a million stars.
She had everything we did not have,
   and so she gave to us
      the singing of her heart
         at Christmastime.

WINTER SKIES

Winter is winning.
The world is gray,
   the ground frozen,
   and all signs of spring hidden.
Inside, the church is crammed with Cassandras,
   their dismal voices
     hovering over once-green land,
      predicting gloom and more gloom.
Only the children see
   that the sky is full
     of angels and of stars.

WORDS

I

Somehow or another
  we found the words to say
  we can't find the words to say
    how we feel.

Reluctantly we turn away,
  each calling for life
    in the other,
  each unable to say
    words of
      affirmation.

It is with joy
  the angels sing
    when one of us
      can find the voice
        to say
          I love you.

II

I want to say to you words
 that have been buried
  deep within me
   unsaid
   unused
 for so long
that, like the shells and rocks
 repeatedly washed
 by sand and sea,
I'm not sure whether the words
 have been destroyed forever
 or polished to their highest shining.
I'll take the risk,
 knowing full well that these words
  living within me
 can find a home within you,
  or be washed forever out to sea.
So listen now
 as I speak to you
  a piece of my heart.

III

We say we don't know how to pray;
our problem is that we never learned to say:
Thank you!
and
I'm sorry!

THE CHURCH

ZACCHAEUS

Zacchaeus,
> small and sinful (according to the Scriptures),
> > didn't want the parade to pass him by.

Zacchaeus,
> little and lost (according to the Scriptures),
> climbed a sycamore tree to see this Jesus.

Zacchaeus,
> chief tax collector and cheat (according to the
> > Scriptures),
> was called by Jesus.

Zacchaeus,
> rich and ready to give (according to the Scriptures),
> gave exuberantly, cheerfully, abundantly.

Zacchaeus,
> sought and saved (according to the Scriptures),
> understood that stewardship is the thank-you of the
> > heart.

According to the Scriptures,
> so do we!

COLD WATER, HOT COFFEE

Sometimes that cup of cold water,
   turns out to be a cup of hot coffee,
and what we're asked to do is
   to pour it . . . and to listen.
Sometimes we Christians
   in our enthusiasm
think we were asked
   to save the world,
when what we were asked to do
   is to go into it
and tell God's story
   to people in need of
some good news.
Anxious activists forget
   that just listening is an act
of compassion.
Driven disciples forget
   that just listening is an act
of faithfulness.
Guilty givers forget
   that just listening is an act
of stewardship.
Since we church people
   have a tendency to be
driven and anxious and guilt-ridden,

perhaps we should
read the directions again
    and pour a cup of hot coffee
and listen
    in His name.

COMMUNION

Gently—like rain on a spring-warm day—
  the words fell
    into my face,
  splashing, rolling, embedding
    in the burrows of my being:
THE BLESSINGS OF CHRIST BE WITH YOU.
There in the midst of broken bread
  in a world of broken bodies
    and splintered spirits
the communion of saints
  became new again,
washed once more
  in blessing and promise.

THE CHURCH IN PROCESS

We in the Church are worshiping Process,
   busily making our lists
     and listing our busy-ness,
   in danger of sacrificing our souls
     for our schedules.
Task-forced,
   agenda-bleary,
     paper-logged,
we look for God in the boardroom
   and salvation in committee.
When process becomes more important
   than people,
it's time to break through
   to the poetry of promise.
It's never too late
   to return to the Poet
     whose sky sings stars
       whose earth dances green
whose promise writes love upon our hearts.

THE CHURCH

The priests and the princes
 are praising process
while the prophets rage
 and the poets weep.
The sheep bleat softly.

The shepherd and staff
 are busy, as scheduled,
but make a note
 to "comfort the sheep"
. . . first thing in the morning.

The priests and the princes
 are still at the altar
in prayer and in praise
 of things as they are.
They're deaf to the bleating.

The prophets have left;
 they camp outside
where they might be heard;
 and the poets have gone
in search of stars.

The sheep have strayed,
   but the shepherd's in committee,
and has no time
   to look for the lost . . .
O Lamb of God, have mercy upon us!

CONFESSION

We confess, O God,
that we don't confess.
Have mercy upon us!

FEEDING SHEEP

He said, "Feed my sheep."
There were no conditions:
    Least of all, Feed my sheep if they deserve it.
    Feed my sheep if you feel like it.
    Feed my sheep if you have any leftovers.
    Feed my sheep if the mood strikes you.
                if the economy's OK . . .
                if you're not too busy . . .
No conditions . . . just, "Feed my sheep."
Could it be that God's Kingdom will come
    when each lamb is fed?
We who have agreed to keep covenant
    are called to feed sheep
        even when it means the grazing will be done
        on our own front lawns.

EYES TO SEE, EARS TO HEAR

They live in used-to-bes
  and cancelled dreams,
    their past gathered in their faces.
What stars they have,
  they plucked from other people's skies,
    and store them now in boxes
      in the basement of the church.
The invitation to the feast
  lies unopened on the altar,
    but their papers are in order.
Doesn't anyone here
  believe in angels or in children?

NO HOPE?

No hope?
Look up into the stars
  or down into a baby's face
and tell me there is no hope. . . .

MY CHURCH FAMILY

Faces and words and glimpses of souls . . .
One by one we come.
We are many,
   and then one.
Precious faces,
   tender words,
      sweet glimpses into souls . . .
Just being here among you is a joy!
Unending thank-yous
   rise within me
for these beloved ones
   within your Church, O God.
Blessed be their lives!
   Blessed be your Church!

MEETINGS

Too much of our time is spent in meetings
  where no meeting takes place.
We arrive and leave as strangers,
  having agreed upon precious little—
  certainly little and not precious.
It's not that we've disagreed
  (oh, that we would care that much!),
  it's just that deciding who will paint
  and who will pay,
  takes a great deal of time,
and none of us has much of that,
  and so we begin to look at our wrists
  and wiggle in our chairs
  and tell each other how busy we are,
  willing to take the time to list,
  for the group to hear,
  just how really bad it is in our shoes
  (the ones that must be moving on any minute now).
When we've assigned a task force and
  moaned about the people who didn't come,
  it's time to go home
  until the next meeting.

O God, where are the Holy Fools?

CHOOSE LIFE

It used to be she had no time for
   eating ice cream cones on frail afternoons
     or wading barefoot through tea parties.
Her time was spent in serious hurry
   and navy-blue practicals
with none left over
   for wrapping rainbows around children's ankles.
When finally she saw
   icicles dancing on the back of winter,
     no one was listening for her clapping.
So . . . now she sits cross-legged in the snow,
   hoping someone will come cartwheeling by
     and touch her cheek.

O God, we shook the dust from our sandals once
   and went on.
Now that the scene's changed,
   are we supposed to go back and get her?

A VARIETY OF GIFTS

The listmakers shake their heads at me
   as Martha shook hers at Mary,
but all's not lost;
   there is hope,
for on the desk
   I found my note:
      water the angel
      type a tree

And they say poets aren't organized!

THIS CHURCH

We don't pretend to understand the mystery
   of what goes on in God's Church.
We just know we feel a pervading spirit of love
   that reaches into the niches of all of us
   and pulls us out into the open,
   free and alive and belonging.
We believe this spirit of love exists because
   God's spirit lives within this Church,
   this unity of persons trying
   to be the Good News.
We see this Church as a circle of persons
   holding hands . . . and dancing . . .
   supporting each other, accepting each other,
   loving each other.
Each person in this dancing circle
   is facing outward . . . reaching into God's world,
   listening for the whimpering,
   watching for the hurting,
   willing to offer a cup of cold water
      in His name.
Sometimes they need the water;
   sometimes you need the water;
   sometimes I need the water.
   Being a part of the Church
   means knowing that
   the cup is always filled
      in His name.

FAITH

A profession of faith is not a part-time promise;
    it's a whole time / all the time / every time way of
      life,
and we who say we believe in Jesus Christ
     are saying
    now and tomorrow and forever.

NEW SHOOTS

Born in the light of the Bright and Morning Star,
  we are new.
Not patched, not mended . . . but new
  like a newborn . . .
  like the morning . . .
The guilt-blotched yesterdays are gone;
  the soul stains are no more!
There is no looking back;
  there are no regrets.
In our newness, we are free.
In the power of God's continuing creation,
  we are:
  new shoots from the root of Jesse,
  new branches from the one true Vine,
  new songs breaking through the world's deafness.
This then is a new day.
New shoots, new branches,
  new songs, new day . . .
Bathed in the promise of God's New Creation,
  we begin!

THE FAITHFUL

Up and up the stairs of time
   the pilgrims climb . . .
      no matter what
one more time
     always one more time.

ASCENSION

Blessing them,
   He ascended into heaven.
Gone, but not gone.
Ascended, but still with us.
Alive among us
Among us
Us!
No longer sad at his leaving,
   we wait in joy and wonder
   for the Spirit.
Blessed,
   we wait to do his bidding,
   to go out to all the world
   to tell the Good News
      that God loves us so much He chose to live among
   us.
Crucified Risen Lord lives still among us.
Lo, He is with us always
       even unto the end of the world . . .
Ascended Lord, ever Emmanuel!

PRAYER OF CONFESSION

O God, we confess that we forget who we are.
We don't listen for a still small voice.
We walk with our heads down
  and miss all the stars that could be ours,
but we know, O God, that you are a God of Hope
  who does not forget your covenant with us,
a Shepherd-God who looks for lost sheep,
a faithful God who keeps calling us
  in spite of our deafness,
a God who enters our history and
  opens our eyes
    and heals our blindness.
O God, accept us as your stewards
  and send us out in the hope
    of your love. Amen.

LITANY OF CONFESSION

LEADER: *O Lord, we've heard the old, old story*
and we confess our sin of indifference.

PEOPLE: God, jolt our lives
to turn and look at You once more.

LEADER: *Give us the ears to hear your amazing story*
that God would become one of us
    living among us
    teaching us
    sitting down at table with us
    breaking bread and drinking wine with us
      and then dying among us
        for us.
Amazing grace!

PEOPLE: O Lord, we ask for your presence this day.
Brush against us when we least expect it.
Touch us with your Spirit.
Take us by the shoulders and shake us awake
    to your incredible truth.

LEADER: *We are your people*
and you are our God.
Forgive our faithlessness, O faithful God!
And see beyond our apathy,

our thoughtlessness
our self-centeredness
our wrong choices.
See into our hearts,
for you are our Treasure.

PEOPLE: We pledge once more to give
to those who need us, that this world might
be more human.
We pledge to do away with indifference.
We pledge to tell the old, old story
  in new life-changing ways!
For Jesus' sake. Amen.

FORGIVE US

O God, you gave us a garden of Eden
  and we chose to wander in deserts of our own making.
You gave us the Light of the world
  and we chose to do our night-crawling.
Forgive us our squandering
  our wandering
    our lack of commitment.
Forget not your covenant with us, O God, and
  choose us still
    to tell your Good News
      to give all that we have
        that all might be one in your Shalom.
      In Jesus' name we pray. Amen.

PRAYER OF THANKSGIVING

O Lord, you flower the gardens for us
  and make green the wastelands.
The mountains burst forth with streams of water
  and the fields are filled with your bounty.
Thank you, God, for all good gifts,
  and make our hearts your home
    that we might serve you all of our days
      and live in the hope of your peace. Amen.

PRAYER OF STEWARDSHIP

O Lord, forgive our fears
    that so stifle our stewardship.
Forgive our giving in and our giving up
    instead of giving ourselves
        to Christ's mission of love.
Remind us that our hope
    is in standing up and risking,
        in taking our stewardship seriously.
Help us to remember, O Lord, that
    the stewardship question is not really,
        How much will we give?
    The stewardship question is,
        How will we spend what we have been given?
We pray it will be faithfully
    and cheerfully.

OUR GIFTS ARE GIFTS OF HOPE

Our yearning after God,
  our hope for a better way
    creates infinite possibilities
      to touch the lives of the untouched

        to reach the hearts
          of the unreached

        to heal the wounds
          of the unhealed

        to feed the bodies
          of the unfed

        to accept the personhood
          of the unaccepted

        to love the being
          of the unloved

Our gifts are gifts of hope;
O God,
  touch
    reach
      heal
        feed
          accept
          and love us
  that we might love one another.

OUR LORD IS CALLED HOPE

Our Lord was a Lord who turned
    things upside down and inside out
    a man who dined with sinners
    a man who befriended prostitutes and tax collectors
    a man who was called heretic
    a man who broke the Sabbath rules
    a man who changed water into wine

And he bids us to follow him
    to turn things upside down and inside out
    to go where the hurting is
    to change water into wine
    to change who we are into the Kingdom of God.

THE WIDOW'S MITE

Frail and stooped with the ravages of illness,
   out of the hospital . . .
      her only yearning: to go to church.
   Out of the hospital
      into the sanctuary . . .
Wearing joy upon her wrinkled face,
   she is full of light.
Her hand shaking, she places her offering on the plate.
O God, a widow's mite!
   This day in this time
      lovingly, cheerfully offered to her Lord . . .
O God, a widow's mite,
   a sign of hope among us!

—Luke 21:1–4

JESUS ENCOUNTERS ZACCHAEUS

O God
  we come before you
    holding our hopes and dreams
      in the pocket of our hearts.

We are so small, O God,
  sometimes we do not see you
    over the crowds that clutter the streets of our lives.
Forgive us, God, for we should go to all lengths to see
    you.
We should climb trees or mountains for a glimpse of
    you.
O Lord,
  Open the door to our hearts;
    come into our homes;
      dine with us!

Take our offering, Lord,
  and make miracles of our hopes and dreams.

—Luke 19:1–9

CASTING OUT THE MONEY CHANGERS

Loud voices
  come from the Temple
wheeling and dealing
  the haggling of those who come to buy
  the clinking of coins
  the sounds of animals and birds
A CACOPHONY OF BLASPHEMY
And into this chaos comes
  the Angry Christ!
    overturning tables of the money changers
    unseating the pigeon sellers
      OUT! OUT! OUT!
    with whip, driving out the blasphemers!

O Lord, once more you speak to the people
  with whom you have entrusted the gospel.
Forgive us, Lord, for filling your church with idols,
  for spending our energy, our time, our talents, our
    money
    in the cacaphony of blasphemy.
We know better, Lord, for your house shall be called a
  house of prayer
Our prayer is that we may use faithfully all that you've
  given us.

—John 2:13–17

69

THE PARABLE OF THE TALENTS

All of us from time to time
  have dug our hiding places
    and buried our songs
    or our silver.
Thinking our voices too weak
  and our offering too meager,
Out of fear
  we have buried our talents.
What bothers us, of course,
    is the reaction to the third servant,
  for Jesus is talking
    directly
    to us,
  the ones who have been entrusted with
    God's Word.
Jesus reminds us
    that it is God's gifts we bury.
  Let us, in this new Church resolve
  to unearth our talents
    and offer unto God all that we have
    and are!

                  —Matthew 25:14–30

THE RICH YOUNG RULER

O God, this scares us,
 for our prayer is often,
  "What can we do, O Lord?"

O God, forgive us
 and don't give up on us.
Forgive us
 our half-hearted stewardship,
Forgive us when we make gods of our money
 or our position
 or our ambition.
Help us to "leave everything"
 and serve no other gods before you.
In the name of Him who we would follow,
 our Lord Jesus Christ, Amen.

—Matthew 19:16–30

"WHERE YOUR TREASURE IS . . . "

O Lord, some of us have mites
  and some of us have millions
    and most of us fall somewhere in between.
We know it's our responsibility to give from what we've
    been given,
  and Jesus made it very clear that
    it was not the size of the gift,
      but the size of the giver's heart that matters.
You, O Lord, know our treasures and our hearts.
May our hearts swell to the occasion!

                                  Matthew 6:19–21

THE HOLY
IN
THE ORDINARY

GOD'S HOLY PEOPLE

Here we are, you and I,
    called to be God's Holy People.
You say you're not the holy type,
    but I'm not talking about holier-than-thou.
        I'm not talking about religious ritual,
and the last thing I mean is self-righteousness!

Jesus chastised the self-righteous,
    the ones who spent their days doing religious things,
the ones who spent so much time in religious ritual
    that they didn't have time for tenderheartedness.

I'm not talking about them;
    I'm talking about us.
I'm talking about paying attention
    to the things Jesus taught people,
        ordinary people, people like you, people like me . . .
Look at the disciples: ordinary people
    called to follow,
        called to be God's Holy People,
called to live in this world with tender hearts.
Live holy lives . . . impossible?
Is anything impossible to God?
That old woman Sarah thought it impossible
    to have a child . . .

The lepers thought it impossible
   to be healed . . .
The disciples thought it impossible
   to feed five thousand with two loaves and
      five fishes . . .
Mary and Martha thought it impossible
   that their brother Lazarus was alive . . .
The lame thought it impossible to walk . . .
The blind thought it impossible to see . . .

Here we are, ordinary people,
   called to be the Holy People of God.
If you have eyes to see and ears to hear,
   see and hear God's holiness in your life.

HOLY GROUND

The ground . . . the ordinary, always present,
  hardly-in-danger-of-extinction ground . . .
and God called it holy!

I know that Moses took off his shoes
  because God told him he was standing on holy
    ground.
What I don't know is,
  When is the ground holy and when is it not?
When do I take off my shoes?

I walk upon the frozen ground in winter,
  and find it cracked and ugly, lacking color.
There's nothing here to make me stop and say,
  "Holy ground,"
yet I know that underneath
  spring is growing,
and in the months to come
  I'll be stopped dead in my tracks
    by crocus and tulip and daffodil
  and in some morning's light
    I'll see a blaze of forsythia
  and a triumph of pink dogwood
    and I'll have a whiff of lemon thyme
and I'll take off my shoes.

When is the ground holy,
   this ground that yields to us Life?
If the earth is the Lord's
   and the fullness thereof,
no amount of planting or tilling or harvesting
   is going to mean the bounty is ours.
We can't earn it;
   everything is a gift.
And the gifts are not unique:
   they're everywhere . . . commonplace . . . ordinary:
ordinary trees, ordinary vegetables,
   ordinary fruits, ordinary flowers . . .
ordinary beauty, ordinary bounty
ordinary extravagant gifts.
Just in case,
   I'll take off my shoes from time to time
and say, "Thank you."

STONES

When those walls came tumbling down,
  the people of Israel
headed for the Jordan.

As soon as the priests
  put their feet in the water,
the river stopped its flow.

With the priests holding
  the Box of the Covenant of the Lord,
the people crossed on dry land.

BUT THEY REMEMBERED TO REMEMBER.

Twelve men carried twelve stones
  so that when their children asked
    they could tell them
what God had done.

Twelve stones were set
  in the middle of the Jordan
    where the priests had stood,
the priests holding
  the Box of the Covenant of the Lord,
    and the people remembered
what God had done.

Was there ever anything as ordinary as a stone?
The land is full of stones;

plentiful, ordinary stones.
Stones on the bank of the Jordan
spilled over into the water—
plentiful, ordinary stones—
but there is an altar of
twelve holy stones
on the bottom of the Jordan,
and there are twelve
holy stones
in the memory of God's people.

Ordinary stones don't speak
and they don't sing,
but holy stones do.

INTO THE ORDINARY

O Amazing God, you come into our ordinary lives
    and set a holy table among us,
filling our plates with the Bread of Life
    and our cups with Salvation.
Send us out, O God,
    with tenderheartedness
to touch an ordinary everyday world
    with the promise of your holiness.

BREAD AND WINE

Ordinary bread made by ordinary people
        is holy
when we take and eat
        and remember.
Ordinary grapes taken by ordinary people
        made into ordinary wine
            is holy
when we hold it to our lips and drink
        and remember.
This bread . . . remember his body was given for us.
This wine . . . remember his blood was poured out for
        us.
Bread and wine,
    from ordinary to holy. . . .
        Remember.

THE MESSIAH

Look for the Messiah where you will,
   but you'll find him where you live.
He will not be separated and kept apart
   from those who cry to him.
He will be found right in the midst
   of the daily, routine, ordinary stuff of life.
So wherever you're living
   look for him.
In the ordinary niches of that living
   look for the holy
      that the holy might be found in you.

BLESSED FEET

"How beautiful upon the mountain
  are the feet of those
    who bring good tidings."
Even feet are holy
  when those are the feet
    that carry good news.
When you go out, remember
  that your feet have holy work to do
    just like the words of your mouth
      and the meditations of your heart.
Go out now and tell what's on your heart
      Tell the good news that God is with us.
      Blessed be your feet.

THE BIRTH

It was an ordinary event;
   after all,
      women give birth every day.
The baby cries;
   the woman puts the child to breast,
   and the world goes on.
God did not pitch a tent among us
   in an extraordinary way.

Jesus arrived as all of us do,
   powerless and dependent,
      a baby.
What ordinary means
   for the Son of God!
No royal robes, no crown,
   nor was there priestly garb!
In fact, there was no garb at all . . .
   just a naked baby
      born to dwell among us . . .

And yet, in that ordinary place,
   holy was the night,
      for holy were the hearts
of those who heard the word of God
   in the ordinary birth cry
      of a child.

WOMEN OF FAITH

SARAH

To begin the presentation, have a group of women (four is enough), dressed in biblical garb, sing the first verse of "Sarah's Circle," by Carole A. Etzler (sung to the tune of "Jacob's Ladder"). At the conclusion of the drama, the four women can reappear and sing the remaining verses, perhaps inviting the audience to sing along.

CHORUS: *(individually calling, slowly, stretching out the word)*
Sa-ra-a-a-h! Sa-ra-a-a-h! Sa-ra-a-a-h!

(Then, all together) You laughed, Sarah!

SARAH: No, I—

CHORUS: Yes, you did, Sarah! You laughed!

SARAH: No . . . I mean, maybe a little bit . . . I didn't really *laugh!*

CHORUS: Sa-ra-a-a-h!

SARAH: All right, so I laughed!

CHORUS: You laughed, all right. You laughed, Sarah, and why not?

SARAH: Why not, indeed! Barren Sarah! . . . I don't know why it's so surprising that I should laugh after all these years of being laughed at!

CHORUS: *(giggles)*

SARAH: Laughter! The laughter began that first year we were married. Have you heard? they whispered. Then louder, snickering when I passed. Sarai is childless. Of course, they were laughing at Abram, too. He was so proud when he married me. I was beautiful then. Not old and wrinkled and barren. I was beautiful and still hopeful. Perhaps when we settled down in Haran—perhaps then I would have a child. After all, God kept telling Abram that he would have many descendants.

I didn't laugh then. I believed. I believed that God would bless me when he blessed Abram. I prayed every night that I might conceive. But it didn't happen. Barren Sarai . . . each day praying that life would stir within me, each day hoping my womb would fill with child. Each day enduring the questions, the assumptions, the laughter. Each day listening to the voices of the children. And the cries of the babies. And the gentle voices of the mothers bent over their young . . . the weeping . . . the hoping . . . the yearning. . . . But I was barren.

I don't know which was worse: the scorn or the pity. What is a woman worth if she cannot give a man a child?

CHORUS: Worthless. A barren woman is worthless.

SARAH: Worthless . . . and yet, Abram always loved me. I don't remember a time he didn't love me.

He has loved me since I was a child. I've always known what I meant to him, and I've never felt that he thought I was worthless. Of course, Abram has always been different from other men. He is faithful to me, for he is faithful to God. He knows how I ache because of the emptiness of my womb. He knows, and he cares somehow, and it is to God and not to me that he said, You have not blessed me with children. Even though I was childless, Abram has always been thankful for me. I know other people don't understand that, but Abram's gratefulness for me and for life and for all that he has (because he is a very wealthy man) . . . this gratefulness comes from his faithfulness. He always says that God is in charge and that God has given us much to be grateful for.

But still I worried, wondering when Abram might turn away from me.

CHORUS: You were sure of Abram's love, but afraid that, in time, he, too, would think you were worthless . . .

SARAH: Well, there was that incident in Egypt. The famine came and we had to move. As I've said, Abram has always been very proud of my beauty. Perhaps in some sense it makes up for my barrenness . . . in Abram's mind. I don't know . . . but when we went to Egypt, he still thought I was beautiful. Beautiful enough to worry about the princes and even Pharaoh himself. So Abram asked me to tell them I was his sister instead of his wife so that they wouldn't kill him. I was beautiful. I was barren. And I felt completely demeaned. He insisted that he was desperate, that they would kill him and then neither of us would escape. "Tell them that you are my sister, and they will treat me well." Beautiful, Barren, and Demeaned. I kept hoping as I walked away to Pharaoh's palace that Abram would stop me, would fight for me, would dare death rather than have me shamed. He looked the other way, and Pharaoh's men led me away. I hurt too much to cry. I was alone, and my husband, whom I had always trusted, gave me away to another man. Alone and barren; I did not feel beautiful. I was nothing. I did no laughing that night.

I fell on my knees and I cried to God. I was nobody, but God heard the sobs of a nobody that night. "What, O God, have I done to deserve this? Am I to be deserted by my husband and now by my God?"

CHORUS: You dared to speak to God like that?

SARAH: I dared to believe that God could do something, and would do something . . . even for a barren, worthless woman. I believed that God could change the situation.

CHORUS: And God heard!

SARAH: And God heard! God heard and saved me. It was then I knew for sure that I belonged to God just as surely as Abram did. I suppose I'd been a little jealous because God was always talking to Abram and choosing Abram for great honors, and Abram was faithful and built God altars all over the countryside. I guess I felt a little left out. What I found out in Egypt was that God was with me . . . with *me* . . . God was with me when I was in darkness and terror. Once I was no one, and now I was God's.

CHORUS: And Abram?

SARAH: I forgave him and God forgave him. And Abram, being Abram, rejoiced in my new understanding of my faith.

CHORUS: But still you were barren.

SARAH: I did not forget my barrenness, I just no longer concentrated on it. I simply did not expect to feel life in my belly. But God kept on telling Abram that he was blessed and that he would have a multitude of descendants. I think even faithful Abram was having a difficult time knowing what God could be thinking, for Abram had no children. I finally came to realize that I would not conceive, and so I went to Abram and told him to take my slave, Hagar, that she might bear a child for me. I felt love for Abram and compassion for him; he did not have a child because I could not conceive. It seemed unfair that he should be punished for my barrenness.

I'm sure people wondered why I had not given a slave to him before. The truth is I could not stand the thought of his being with another woman. That night I wept until Abram came to me in the dark of the night and held me until morning. "It is you I love, Sarai." I believed him, and everything would have been all right if it hadn't been for the attitude of that wretched slave girl. As soon as Hagar knew that she had conceived, she began to be sullen, and then to disobey my orders, and then she asked who was I to give her orders,

I who was unable to give Abram a child
. . . why was I to give orders to the one who
was woman enough to carry that child even
as we spoke.

I couldn't believe how cruel she was, how ut-
terly arrogant and cruel! She taunted me, saying, "How does it feel to know that I am
carrying his child next to my heart?" She
talked about the child constantly, trying to
get a reaction from me. She looked down on
me, telling me I was nothing because I could
not conceive. I lost all judgment and ran to
Abram. I told him it was his fault. I was
trying to get a child for him and now the slave
girl was insolent and treated me despicably.

I was surprised at his answer. "She's your slave.
Do what you want with her" (Gen. 16:6,
TEV). I knew then that I had no reason to be
jealous as far as Abram was concerned. He
was not attached to her emotionally. But I
was not going to have her insolence. Perhaps
I was a little harsh, but as far as I'm concerned she deserved every bit of it.

HAGAR: Maybe I did say some things Sarai didn't like,
but they were all the truth. She is nothing!
Any woman who can't give her husband a
child is nobody. After all, it was her idea that
I carry a child for her! I was doing her a favor.
I didn't want to do it. I knew she'd be jealous.
Don't you think for a moment that Abram
hadn't noticed me. She'd seen him looking at
me. Maybe she was beautiful once, but now
she's old and will never have a child. I am
younger and stronger and I carried Abram's
only child. I have everything she always
wanted, and she can't stand to think about it!

94

She beat me for weeks. Every time I spoke she screamed that she did not have to listen to the obscenities that come out of a slave's mouth. She'd gone mad! Mad with jealousy because I was going to bear Abram's child.

So I ran away . . . into the desert, not knowing where I could go, how I could survive. I really didn't care, so blinded I was with the rage of this oppression! What had I done to be treated like an animal? Was it not enough to be in slavery? To be taken from my family into a foreign country? To be stripped of my customs and my culture, and then, when I am with child, to be treated so harshly?

I expected no answer to my questions. I expected to die there, unable to give birth to my child. I expected nothing. Slaves are nobodies . . . but into the desert, where I sat weeping, came God. I saw God . . . God who sees and does not turn away.

. . . And God changed me from a nobody into a somebody there on the road to Shur. And I got up and returned to Sarai to serve her. And somehow God changed Sarai, too, because when I returned she was weeping that she had driven me away. When I gave birth to Abram's son, Sarai was beside me. But that was thirteen years ago, before God gave Abram his new name . . . Abraham.

SARAH: God gave me a new name, too.

CHORUS: Does a new name change the barrenness of a woman?

SARAH: Is anything too hard for the Lord?

CHORUS: We thought you laughed at the idea, Sarah. . . .

SARAH: Last night I laughed. I know who I am. I am old and my periods have stopped. My womb is shriveled within me. I know who I am and so I laughed. Abraham laughed, too. He is old and he knows I am old. Abraham laughed, but later I found him outside counting the stars to see how many descendants we were going to have. I know who I am, but, more important, I know who God is.

God is the one who is with me, even in the darkness and despair of my life. God is the one who changes what cannot be changed.

I will feel life in my belly after all. I will give Abraham a child in his old age. God is good. I go now to count the stars.

The four women who opened the presentation can now reappear and invite the group to sing all the verses of "Sarah's Circle," if desired. *

---

*A recording of "Sarah's Circle" may be found on the album "Sometimes I Wish" (Atlanta: Sisters Unlimited, 1976).

RAHAB

(Sing:)
Joshua fit the battle of Jericho, Jericho, Jericho,
Joshua fit the battle of Jericho,
   and the walls came tumblin' down.

I built a wall once.
   I built it tall so nobody could get in.
   The trouble was, I couldn't get out.

Walls . . . there are many walls (begin building a wall of
   boxes):
Walls built around a city or a house
   to protect the ones who live there,
walls built to protect against the weather or the wind or
   the sea,
walls built for privacy and walls built as ornament.
And there are the walls we build around ourselves
   to keep the world out
      or to keep the face of God from our window.

I built a wall once.
I built it tall so nobody could get in.
The trouble was, I couldn't get out.

The walls of Jericho were twelve to fourteen feet thick.
   BUT THE WALLS CAME TUMBLING DOWN.
They were built to protect;
   they were built against invasion.

So many tribes, so many peoples
    wanting to conquer us.
Build the walls . . . thick thick double walls;
    build the walls and keep the others out.
Build the walls . . . indestructible walls . . .
    BUT THE WALLS CAME TUMBLING DOWN.
Rumors . . .
    a horde of invaders camping right across the Jordan
      River;
Fear . . . oh, the fear . . . close the city gate!
There are rumors of spies . . .

The king of Jericho—
    he heard the rumors . . .
      what did the king hear?
    The king of Jericho heard—
      the king of Jericho knew
        that spies were in the city.
      Go to Rahab; find the spies.

Oh, Rahab, where are the spies?
—Spies? Those men were spies?
    Those men are gone
      gone before the gate closed
      they left at sundown
      hurry and you'll catch them
      hurry after spies

Rahab, the prostitute:
    she hid the spies.
Up on the rooftop slept the two spies.
Rahab knew the walls would come tumbling down.
Rahab had seen
        seen through the walls
          through the walls in her heart
          through the walls in her home
          through the walls of Jericho
Rahab had seen through all the walls that surrounded
    her.

Rahab had seen the hand of God
  reaching out to tumble those walls.
Rahab knew that the hand that divided the Red Sea
  could tumble the walls of Jericho.

Once a day for six days
  Joshua and his soldiers
    and the priests carrying the Covenant Box
      marched around the city of Jericho.
Seven priests, sounding their trumpets,
  led the procession
    around the city of Jericho
      once a day for six days.

The seventh day,
  the procession marched
    around the city
      One Two Three Four Five Six times
        six times around the city of Jericho.
The seventh time around,
  at the sound of the trumpets
    the soldiers shouted:
  "The Lord has given us the city!"
AND THE WALLS CAME TUMBLING DOWN! *(boxes tumble)*
Only Rahab and her family were saved.

What you may not know is this:

In Hebrews 11 is the beautiful litany of faith.
To have faith is to be sure of the things we hope for,
  to be certain of the things we cannot see.
It was by faith that people of ancient times won God's
  approval.
It is by faith that we understand that the universe was
  created by God's word, so that what can be seen was
  made out of what cannot be seen.
It was faith that made Abel offer to God a better
  sacrifice than Cain's.
It was faith that kept Enoch from dying.

It was faith that made Noah hear God's warnings about things in a future he could not see.

It was faith that made Abraham obey when God called him to go out to a country which God had promised to give him. It was faith that made Abraham able to become a father, even though he was too old and Sarah was unable to have children. And it was faith that made Abraham offer his son Isaac to be sacrificed.

It was faith that made Isaac offer blessings for the future to Jacob and Esau.

It was faith that made Jacob bless each of the sons of Joseph before he died.

It was faith that made Joseph, when he was about to die, speak of the departure of the Israelites from Egypt, and leave instructions about what should be done with his body.

It was faith that made Moses leave Egypt without being afraid of the king's anger.

It was faith that made the Israelites able to cross the Red Sea as if on dry land.

It was faith that made the walls of Jericho fall down after the Israelites had marched around them for seven days.

And it was faith that kept the prostitute Rahab from being killed with those who disobeyed God . . .

Rahab, the Canaanite . . .

   Rahab, the prostitute . . .

      Rahab, a woman . . .

         listed with the faithful ancestors.

What you may not know is that Rahab is the mother of Boaz who married Ruth. Rahab is listed in Matthew 1 in the lineage of Jesus.

All of us good church people know the story
of how Joshua "fit the battle of Jericho."
But few of us remember Rahab.
The Sunday school lessons

avoid ignore remain silent about
this woman who (along with God)
made the whole strategy possible.
Sometimes God's choices leave us
 a little baffled, a little embarrassed.
Why a harlot?
Surely there was in Jericho some goodworks woman
 who had lived a nearly saintly life . . .
                    BUT
The churched and the chaste
 are not always God's choices.
God reads hearts rather than position papers
 on the state of our virtue.
It always makes me a little nervous
 when God makes these unlikely choices.
Perhaps we in the church should appoint a task force
 to be sure that we're the wall tumblers
   rather than the wall builders.

(Sing:)
"Rahab fit the battle of Jericho, Jericho, Jericho . . .
Rahab fit the battle of Jericho,
and the walls came tumblin' down."

GOMER

A monologue by Hosea's wife, Gomer.

(Gomer enters from the back of the room and walks slowly, looking at the people in the audience. She is over-dressed: lots of jewelry . . . perhaps chewing gum . . . heavy make-up. She arrives at the podium [if one will be used] in front and pauses and looks directly out at the people.

What are you staring at? . . . What's a matter? Haven't you church people ever seen a harlot before? . . . Yeah, my name's Gomer; I'm the one. *(Looks at a woman directly.)* You got a good look, honey?

Yeah; I know. My reputation precedes me, as they say. . . . Listen, there's two sides to every story. You know what I mean?

Listen, I was just minding my own business. OK, so it wasn't the best business in the world. You think I would have chosen it if I had any other way to make a living?

Well, as I was saying, here I was minding my own business when one of the girls says that some guy wanted to see me. Well, that's not so unusual, so I went out—and what was unusual was that here was this . . . this . . . this nabi! That's a prophet, to you. Everybody knows they're crazy. Usually they're on the street corners and they'd never speak a direct word to any of us, but this one wasn't on the street corner and he was here and he had asked for me. I thought it was peculiar, but I then thought, so he's not what he seems!

I look him in the eye and I tell him that I'm expensive. You know what he answered, this nabi? He said, that's all right; I'm going to pay you the rest of your life. Well, you can imagine what I thought . . . uh-oh, a looney!

I was trying to get rid of him when he said he wanted to marry me. Well, right then and there, I saw my way out of this rotten business. I mean, at that point, I had no idea just how crazy Hosea was. That's his name, Hosea. As my so-called friends said, You shoulda known he was crazy, Gomer; he wanted to marry you. Yeah, that *was* crazy, 'cause he was a righteous person. Of course, at that point I didn't know just how righteous he was. So I said, what the heck, and followed him home.

At first he wasn't half bad, you know? He wasn't bad looking, really. He was sweet, and I wasn't used to that. I was used to being thrown around . . . abused, even. Yeah, you ladies don't know the half of it. So, at first, I wasn't complaining.

Of course, when he told me that it was God who had told him to marry a harlot, I was a little upset. Actually, I was a lot upset. In fact, I was hysterical! But he tried to reassure me, telling me he wasn't crazy and that he really loved me. I think he did love me . . . right from the start. I don't know why. He had never even known anyone like me. He was used to good people. He knew women like . . . well, like you ladies.

At first, he didn't talk about God in every breath, but then when I got pregnant he was overjoyed. He literally ran around the house shouting: Praise the Lord! The Lord's name be praised! Praise the Lord! It is as the Lord said! You are with child!

To tell you the truth, I wasn't all that excited about being with child. I'd never been with child before and I wasn't sure what life was going to be like with a little child around all the time. It was bad enough having Hosea around all the time, looking over my shoulder. Now I had to think about a child.

When it happened, when I gave birth to the child, I was ecstatic. I was surprised at how ecstatic I was. I mean, Hosea was the one usually given to ecstasy! But here I was, as proud as I could be. For the first time in my life, I had done something significant. I looked at that little life in my arms and I felt . . . I've never told anyone this before . . . I felt moved to prayer.

So I thanked God for my child, that my child was a son, that he was whole and well and was, at least to me, absolutely perfect! And then I had to laugh at myself. I sounded just like all the other mothers, but it was a good feeling. I was like all the other women; I had a family now.

Unfortunately, Hosea burst my bubble! When it came to naming the child, Hosea named him "Jezreel." What kind of a name is that for a child, I asked? Hosea answered that it is the name that God had given our son. I asked why God would name our son "Jezreel" and Hosea said that it was because God wanted the people to know (God was always telling Hosea what God wanted the people to know). This time God wanted the people to know that it would not be long before God would punish the king of Israel for the murders that his ancestor Jehu committed at Jezreel. "I am going to put an end to Jehu's dynasty," God said, "and at Jezreel Valley I will at that time destroy Israel's military power."

Well, I was furious! The very idea! God and Hosea, using this little baby as a messenger to God's people! How would you like it if *your* little baby was named Jezreel?

Little did I know when I was well off! I should have left while I was ahead, but when I got really upset, Hosea would be so loving and so sweet and so considerate, I would feel like a princess. Well, anyway . . . I didn't leave . . . not then.

Jezreel was still a baby when I found out I was pregnant again! I had a temper tantrum, of course. Well, that's the way I am; what you see is what you get!

Hosea soothed me and loved me and was so sweet that I calmed down again. You must admit that Hosea was trying to be a good husband and, for the first time in my life, I had something to try for. I wanted to be a good wife, even if I was married to a crazy nabi, and I wanted to be a good mother even if it was to a baby named "Jezreel"!

This time I gave birth to a girl. She was the most beautiful little thing I'd ever seen . . . pink skin that looked like a flower . . . so little and helpless and dependent on me. I was her mother and this little person needed me, and Jezreel, with a name like that, needed me, and Hosea, as strong as he was, said he needed me . . . me! a harlot!

Now, we would have been all right except that God butted in and told Hosea to name my precious little girl "Unloved"! I figured that not only had Hosea gone crazy, but God had gone crazy, too! Why would anybody name a little girl "Unloved"?

I said to Hosea: "I suppose this is foolish to ask, but why would God name my baby 'Unloved'?" He looked exasperated. "Gomer, why can't you understand that I am a prophet and God's messenger? Don't you understand how wonderful it is to be chosen by God to be God's messenger?"

Somehow, it escaped me! "Hosea," I said, "nobody names their children these strange names. 'Unloved' is a horrible name. She's gonna grow up to be a neurotic!"

"God told me," says Hosea. I pouted.

I should have pouted longer. I had no sooner weaned "Unloved" than I got pregnant again. Yes, I know . . . you'd think I would have learned! Well, there was something about Hosea that hooked me every time. You know, I think I had fallen in love with that prophet. And that scared me! All the years before I met Hosea, I used men just as they used me. Now I felt something for a man for the first time. It frightened me.

When the baby was born, right away, I asked Hosea: "Well, what odd name does God have for this one?" His answer? "The child's name will be 'Not My People.' "

Well, you can judge me if you like. You can say that you

would have been long-suffering; you would have continued to be faithful. But I had had it!

Can you imagine going to the back door and calling your children in to supper: Jezreel! Unloved! Not My People! It was a joke! The people laughed at Hosea; they looked down on me and they made fun of my children. Yes, I had had it. As soon as "Not My People" was old enough, I left. I didn't want to stick around to take them to the psychiatrist.

And Hosea really didn't love me, after all. The only thing Hosea loved was his righteousness. He was always so right! Gomer, do this . . . Gomer, do that . . . Gomer, a righteous woman would do it this way . . . oh, I wanted to scream. I wanted to be loved by a man just for myself! I was jealous of the time that Hosea spent with God. It was "God this" and "God that" and "God said this" and "God said that." I left!

I went to the temple of Baal. At least Baal didn't mock me. I don't mind telling you that I was beautiful in my youth. The lovers paid handsomely. They bought me gifts of grain and olive oil, linen and wool, gold and silver. I had all the luxuries a woman could want, and none of the headaches of living with a crazy prophet who shouted on street corners that the people should repent!

I lived it up. I dressed in the finest. My lovers brought me presents and treated me like a queen, but in off hours I would sit and wonder what my babies were doing. I would conjure up Hosea's face, handsome and gentle; but then his features would turn judging and demanding and I would be glad I had left. I couldn't stand that judgmental tone he got in his voice. He didn't really love me; he just loved being right!

At certain moments I would wonder where he was . . . was he thinking of me? What were my babies doing? Who was caring for them? . . . Oh, but I couldn't afford to think of them . . . it was too painful.

Then one day I saw a familiar figure speaking to the man in charge at the temple. He was paying him silver and seven bushels of barley. It was Hosea. He came and took my hand

106

and said, "Gomer, I love you. I have bought you back and I will take you home to your children. You will have to wait for me for a long time. During this time you cannot be a prostitute nor can you commit adultery. I will be waiting for you, too. When you can turn again to me, I will be ready to receive you."

Well, you've had a look at me. You know what I am. You know that I'm no prize. I'm anything but a righteous woman. And yet, he loves me. He waits for me, Gomer. Can you imagine a love any grander than that? Can you imagine a love more forgiving?

I do know a good thing when I see it. Hosea is willing to erase all that I have done and forget it. He learned this from his God. Need I say that now Hosea's God is my God, and I intend to be faithful . . .

MARY AND MARTHA
Luke 10:38–41

The play should be performed without props or with a minimum of props. With a little imagination and humor, its message will come through. Enjoy it!

SCENE 1

MARTHA: Mary, Jesus is coming in less than an hour. Give me a hand with this sweeping, will you?

MARY: *(who has been looking out the "door" for* Jesus, *turning to* Martha*)* Martha, we've already swept the floor!

MARTHA: Well, we missed something . . . look in this corner!

(Mary *rolls her eyes and shrugs her shoulders and takes the worn broom and sweeps half-heartedly. In a few seconds, she runs back to look out the door again.* Martha *looks up from her very vigorous dusting and scolds her sister.*)

MARTHA: Mar-r-r-r-y!

(Mary *swings the broom a few more times. In a few seconds* Martha *drops to her knees and*

108

begins to scrub the floor where they've swept.
She wipes her brow and scrubs harder. Mary
goes back to the door and lingers there, look-
ing out. Martha *finally rises and speaks to*
Mary *again.*)

MARTHA: Mary, we've got to set the table.

(Both women go to a cupboard and get dishes
out and carry them to the table, which is very
low because the diners sit on cushions on the
floor. Martha *turns for more dishes and* Mary
returns to the door. Martha *continues to fuss*
over the table, arranging and rearranging the
pottery pieces, shaking her head and deciding
to put them elsewhere, and so on.)

MARTHA: Mary, go get some flowers for the table, will
you?

MARY: Oh, Martha, that would be lovely! I'll get them
out back.

*(*Mary *exits and* Martha *stares at the table. She*
makes one final adjustment to a dish. Mary
re-enters and Martha *reaches for a vase for the*
flowers and hands it to Mary, *who puts the*
vase in the middle of the table while Martha
goes for water. She pours it carefully into the
vase. Mary *plops the flowers into the vase,*
smiles, and hurries back to the door to watch
for Jesus. Martha *looks very hard at the vase*
and then meticulously rearranges the flowers.
Satisfied, she goes to the back of the stage,
where she makes a fire, puts five pots over the
fire one by one, and then begins making bread.
She takes a bowl, pours flour into it, pours
water from a pitcher, mixes and kneads the
bread, and finally leaves it to rise. All the
while, Mary *is looking for* Jesus. Martha

109

again begins to clean up, putting away things,
wiping up, and sweeping.)

MARY: There he is! There he is! Oh, Martha, there's
Jesus! He's coming right this minute!

(Mary *jumps up and down and whirls herself*
around the room. Martha *immediately drops*
to her knees and scrubs for a second, and then
rushes back to the table and rearranges the
flowers again, moves a plate, and then goes to
the back of the stage and picks up the bread
and puts it in the oven. She is not at the door
to welcome Jesus *when he enters.*)

MARY: Come in! Come in! Shalom, Jesus!

(Mary *welcomes* Jesus *with a kiss and* Martha
comes rushing out and also welcomes him
with a kiss, then rushes back to get a bowl and
towel to wash his feet. Mary *leads* Jesus *in to*
sit down and she sits beside him. Martha
washes his feet. Mary, *sitting beside* Jesus,
looks very rapt and listens to him talk. The
audience doesn't hear him, but Jesus *moves*
his head and maybe his hands while "speak-
ing" and Mary *nods, and so on. Meanwhile,*
Martha *goes back to the "kitchen" and stirs*
and slices and chops, rushing back and forth
to the table, taking bread from the oven, carry-
ing pot after pot to the table, back and forth,
back and forth. After a few minutes of this,
have someone play some "rushing" music on
the piano. Jesus *and* Mary *are oblivious, deep*
in conversation. Finally, exasperated, Martha
moves toward Jesus *and* Mary.)

MARTHA: Lord, don't you care that my sister has left me
to do all the work by myself? Tell her to come
and help me!

110

JESUS: Martha, Martha! You are worried and troubled over so many things, but just one is needed. Mary has chosen the right thing, and it will not be taken from her [TEV].

(Martha *hangs her head and her shoulders slump.* Mary *gets up and puts her arm about* Martha *and leads her to the table, beckoning* Jesus *to join them. The three barely sit down when* Martha *throws up her hands.*

MARTHA: I forgot the wine!

(Martha *starts to get up, but* Mary *gently gestures for her to sit.* Mary *gets and pours the wine. The three sit, bow their heads, and then begin to eat, smile, and "chat." Then* Jesus *gets up and leaves.*)

SCENE 2

(Both sisters are sitting on pillows in the middle of their house.)

MARTHA: I ruined it all!

MARY: Now, Martha, you're still upset and you're very tired. Why don't you get some rest? You'll feel better in the morning.

MARTHA: I could never sleep! I'll never sleep again! Here I wanted it to be so perfect and, as it turned out, I was so irritable, I behaved terribly! Do you think he'll ever forgive me?

MARY: Oh, Martha, he wasn't angry with you. I think he was gently telling you that you just didn't understand. You were so anxious to do something for Jesus that you wore yourself out entertaining when actually he didn't care a bit about a big elegant dinner. One dish would have been enough.

MARTHA: But how did you know, Mary? Doesn't hospital-ity mean doing all you can to make your guest feel welcome?

MARY: Exactly, but the thing that makes Jesus feel most welcome is for us to take the time to listen and to care about what he's telling us.

MARTHA: But I do care. I was going to listen as soon as dinner was over.

MARY: I know, Martha, but had you chosen a simpler meal, you would have had more time to listen and you wouldn't have been so tired that you couldn't hear.

MARTHA: Oh, now I'm going to go down in history as the too-fussy hostess, the one so caught up in entertaining that she didn't have time to lis-ten to Jesus! Everybody's going to know that Jesus chastised me for being too fastidious, and commended you for making the right choice! Oh, I'm just miserable!

MARY: Oh, Martha, everybody will know that Jesus loves you just as he loves me and Lazarus. You were rebuked in love because Jesus doesn't want you to miss out on his teachings. He was telling us what is important in life so that we and others can have life abundant.

MARTHA: I can see it now! It's going to be Mary and Martha, the good one and the bad one!

MARY: Martha! I bet there will even be some sermons on your loving action in preparing Jesus' sup-per and on my inconsiderateness. There will probably be some women's association circles named after us.

MARTHA: Yeah, the Martha Circle will be the busy-busy-bodies!

MARY: No! The Martha Circle will be the ones who get things done, who go for action! And the Mary Circle will be the ones who study.

MARTHA: Well, if that's true, they'll miss the point, for you acted, too. We both acted; it was just that I acted needlessly while you gave priority to listening to Jesus.

MARY: Well, we won't be there to interpret ourselves to them. Surely they'll put themselves in our sandals and know that we were both loved by Jesus and that on this particular evening, Jesus was teaching us and them about making choices about how we spend our lives. Speaking of choices, I think we ought to go to bed and get some rest!

MARTHA: Well, not without cleaning up first!

THEY BROUGHT THE WOMAN
BEFORE JESUS
John 8:1–11 (TEV)

This presentation can be given with the Reader alone or with the Reader and two people, one portraying Jesus and the other, the Woman. The congregation or group is a very important part of this reading. The first request that the Reader makes is to invite the group into the Temple. The Reader should explain that the men in the group need to move to the front of the room and the women must be behind the men. Then, just before the reading begins, explain that the men will need to go get the woman and drag her into the Temple before Jesus. If it is a large group, it's not necessary that all the men go out and come back in with the woman; just indicate to some of the men that it is time for them to go get her.

When the time comes for "muttering" and "grumbling," the Reader can again indicate to the entire group that they are to "mutter" and "grumble" when it is appropriate. It will not be necessary to wait for long for people to get accustomed to this; I've found most are quite willing to join in. When the accusers leave and the Temple is emptied, indicate to the group that they are to leave (go to the back of the room). If it is a large group, again, only a representative number need get up and go (perhaps the same group that brought the woman in). Jesus and the Woman speak only where it is written in, but they can "act" as the script indicates. This should be a dramatic reading, without much movement of either Jesus or the Woman.

The woman caught in adultery . . .
The woman was caught in the act of adultery.
That's what they said, the men,
     the Teachers of the Law and the Pharisees,
   the men who brought her into the Temple
   and made her stand in front of the crowd that had
     gathered
     to listen to Jesus.
They said she was caught in the very act of committing
     adultery,
   and here she was standing in the Temple
     before Jesus and her accusers
     and the crowd that had gathered to listen to Jesus.

Now the law of Moses says she must die.
The law of Moses says that any woman caught
   in the act of adultery
     must be stoned
        to death.
What do you say, Jesus?

What do you say, Jesus?
What can you say, Jesus?
You certainly won't disagree with the law of Moses!
   And yet, if you don't,
   you challenge Roman authority . . .
   to say nothing of
   going against your teachings of compassion.
What will it be, Jesus?
Break the Law or kill the woman?

I've always found it strange
   downright confounding
that a woman was caught in the act of adultery
   but the man was not.
Those who caught them,
those sent to catch them,

let the man go free.
Yet, the law of Moses says
both man and woman caught in adultery
   will be put to death
      stoning death.
Where was the man?
Why was he not dragged before Jesus, too?
Could it be that the man was a friend of the accusers?
Or of someone in authority?
Someone who did not have to obey the rules?
Where was the man?
Did the accusers look the other way,
   assuming that the woman was the seducer?
Boys will be boys
   and men will be men
      and women will be stoned to death?
I've always found it strange that the shame
   belongs to the woman;
      the woman, whose shame can only be blotted out
        by death.
So say the men who brought the woman
   who stood before Jesus in the Temple.
Whatever the reasons, the man went free,
   leaving the woman to bear the shame
      alone in the Temple in front of the crowd
        and before Jesus.
What do you say, Jesus?

What can you say, Jesus?
To the Scribes and Pharisees who caught the woman,
   and who are even more anxious to catch Jesus . . .
Let him dispute the Law of Moses!
Ha! We've got him now!
The Teachers and the Pharisees who quoted Moses
   figured they could catch this one
      who taught in the Temple,
   this Jesus from Nazareth

who had captured the imagination of the people.
They figured they could discredit him
  in front of the people.
What do you say, Jesus?
Break the Law
  or let the woman die?

The Temple filled with people
  who waited in silence
    for Jesus to speak.
But Jesus said nothing.
Instead, he bent over and wrote on the ground.
They waited for his answer,
  his answer to the trick question,
    but Jesus bent over and wrote on the ground.
Necks strained.
  Throats cleared.
    What did he write on the ground?
What did he write on the ground
  in front of the Scribes and the Pharisees and the
    crowd
    and the woman who was caught in the act of
      adultery?
The accusers began to grumble
  and the crowd began to mutter
    and the woman stood still in silence
while Jesus wrote on the ground.
The mumbling and the muttering
  echoed throughout the Temple.
Writing on the ground! Why doesn't he answer?
What's your answer, Jesus of Nazareth?
Set aside the Law of Moses
  and the people will turn away from you;
Condone the Law and you challenge the Romans
  and the woman dies,
    the woman caught in adultery.
What do you say, Jesus?

117

Amid the muttering and the grumbling,
   Jesus stood up,
     and said:
   "Whichever one of you has committed no sin
     may throw the first stone."
Silence . . . no movement . . . silence.
Jesus bent down again
   and began writing once more on the ground.
One by one the accusers left.

When Jesus stood again,
   all were gone
     except for the woman caught in adultery.
Jesus asked: "Where are they?
           Is there no one left to condemn you?"
The woman answered: "No one, sir."

No one! No one . . . no one . . . no one . . .
No one left to condemn!
   Unless, of course . . . Jesus. . . .
The woman could have left when the others left;
   she could have slipped away.
After all, the accusers had.
She could have fled while she had the chance,
   but she waited to hear what the Teacher had to say.
In obedient silence she waited.
And then the words came:
   "Well, then . . . I do not condemn you either.
   "Go, but do not sin again."

The woman caught in adultery was freed.
She would not die . . .
   not a stone had been hurled at her . . .
   not a stone had been picked up!
     She was free from death!
Had she left with the others,
   she would have been overjoyed

at her freedom . . . from death.
But she lingered, wanting something more;
   and Jesus, who read her heart, gave it to her.
He gave her what she wanted:
   the real freedom of forgiveness.
She was not only freed, but forgiven—
   forgiven from the death she had chosen,
      forgiven and freed to live again.

The woman was caught in the very act of adultery,
   but she met Jesus
      who forgave her and freed her
         to live again.
Now there is no record of any conversion
   of the woman caught in adultery,
because the woman is hardly the point of the story.
The story is called, "The Woman Caught in Adultery,"
   but it should be called:
      "The Accusers Caught in the Very Act of
         Self-Righteousness."
The woman caught in adultery was forgiven and freed.
The accusers caught in self-righteousness
   did not have her courage.
They didn't stick around to hear
   the verdict on their sins;
neither were they freed . . .
nor were they forgiven.
In their hard-heartedness,
      they continued to choose death
         instead of life.

Happy the woman who is forgiven and freed,
      for she has chosen life.

CLAUDIA
Matthew 27:19

This is a dramatic monologue by Claudia, the wife of Pilate. There is a sentence in Matthew 27:19 that concerns her and a disturbing dream she had of the innocence of Jesus. I have included a small bit of historical information about Claudia in the monologue, but for the most part this piece is a fictionalized account of Claudia's thoughts while Pilate was involved in the trial of Jesus. It is a "might-have-been." In our congregation, we used it on an evening during Lent in the sanctuary with very few lights.

Have you never had a dream that clutched you? Clutched you and held you . . . tossed you and turned you . . . horrified you, its fingers unrelentingly digging into your flesh, burning you with the terror that what you have dreamed is not of this world? A dream so terrifying that you awake trembling, for you know not what is dream and what is reality? You awake and you shiver in the dark and cold night and you wish for morning, for you fear you will never sleep peacefully again.

Such a dream I had last night. So horrendous was it that my own screaming awoke me, and I found my pillow soaked with my tears. My heart seemed stuck in my throat; my pulse would not quiet. Terrified, I paced this palace floor for hours, finally falling exhausted on my bed . . . and then I slept. In the early hours of the day, I slept, slept like the dead, oblivious to the morning's sun or even the crow of the cock. . . .

Of all mornings not to be awake! Of all mornings not to be able to speak to Pilate before he left! This morning above all mornings! I could have warned him! I could have explained the dream. I could have pleaded for the life of this Jesus of Nazareth!

But he's gone. Pilate's already gone to the praetorium. For all I know he may already be trying the Nazarene!

Oh, Pilate! Pilate, be careful! Things are not as they seem!

If only Herod had tried Jesus! He should have! After all, Jesus is from Galilee—but Herod is far too smart for that! So he sent him back to Jerusalem and to Pilate!

Or Caiaphas! If the Sanhedrin had tried him, Pilate wouldn't be right in the middle of it all! But Caiaphas is as clever as Herod. He declared it a civil case and dumped it in Pilate's lap so that Pilate would have to be the one to decide the fate of Jesus.

Oh, Pilate, I wish you were as shrewd as Herod or Caiaphas. I so fear you will let your ambition blur your vision!

Pilate has never been known as a mediator. He is a soldier, and a good soldier, but he has a tendency to settle disputes by sending in his soldiers. Oh, he's learned a lot over the years, but he still bases his decisions on the reaction of Rome. He's simply not the most diplomatic of men!

Even with me, he can't learn to be tactful. For instance, a few days after we had arrived in Jerusalem from Caesarea, and while we were talking about this man named Jesus whom all of Jerusalem was talking about, Pilate reared back in his chair and said to me, "Claudia, stay in your quarters tomorrow. The Nazarene is going to enter Jerusalem and I don't want you to be seen in the streets."

Stay in my quarters! Does Pilate forget that I am the daughter of the third wife of Tiberius and that I am the granddaughter of Caesar Augustus? Stay in my quarters, indeed! I don't need to be told about politics! Pilate knows very well that I know how to be discreet. I know, far better than Pilate, how to behave as ruler of conquered peoples. After all, that's why Pilate married me.

Yes, ours was an arranged marriage, but I must say one that did not displease me. Pilate was young and strong and ambitious. He was well liked by the people because of his reputation as a brave and skillful soldier. His ambition and courage and my connections and know-how made us a perfect combination. We were a team. We've always discussed politics and Pilate's always asked my opinion, with this unspoken question: What, Claudia, do you think Tiberius will think? Pilate makes the decisions, but he does listen to what I have to say.

Oh, Pilate, too, has royal blood; however, several generations ago, the family fell out of favor and lost prestige. They became chief equestrians. Chief equestrian is not a bad position, but Pilate wanted more . . . a great deal more . . . and, married to me, he could get it. So Tiberius made the expected appointment: Pilate would be prefect of Judea. It was a small post, but one from which Pilate would be expected to move to larger responsibilities.

When we first moved to our palace in Caesarea, I thought we complemented each other, but I had not known—nor, fortunately, had Tiberius—how very much Pilate despised the Jews. He thinks their religion is superstitious; it's all right for women, but men should find power in money and position and the sword. Pilate finds the infighting and the petty arguments over legalisms quite distasteful. "They're always bickering," he said to me one evening. "They cry blasphemy at one another constantly, and what groveling they do in front of their God! I bow only to Rome!"

The ironic thing is that if Pilate had kept his feelings under control we wouldn't have even been here when Jesus arrived in Jerusalem. With a little tact, Pilate could have solved the civil problems of the province, dealt with the Jews firmly but fairly, and pleased Tiberius so much that he would have promoted him. Pilate, however, almost immediately made himself an enemy of the Jews. Wanting to show them who was in charge, he equipped his soldiers with medallions of the emperor, throwing into their faces his lack of respect for their religion, which forbids graven images.

Pilate desperately wanted to advance his career, to be known for his ability to rule and for his allegiance to Rome, and he did quite well for some time after the medallion incident. I was pleased with his dedication to peace and the fair way he began to deal with the people. He suppressed his hatred of the Jews and word of his good work reached Rome.

Then he got an idea: He would build an aquaduct. It sounded promising. Surely Rome would sit up and take notice. I encouraged Pilate in his plans. This was just the sort of project that would advance him and might even get us a more prominent post. Everything went well, I thought, until one evening a group of red-faced, tight-lipped Sanhedrin appeared at our door, angrily shouting at Pilate. Pilate had used Temple tax money to build the aquaduct!

It was shortly after that that I met Joseph . . . Joseph of Arimethea. He was a member of the council, a devout Jew and a good man, judging from all that I had heard. I decided to learn all I could about the Jewish religion, to show an interest, so that perhaps the people would think Pilate, too, was interested.

Joseph told me of their God . . . a God who had made covenant with them . . . a God who cared about their everyday lives. I had never heard of such a god. My gods had always been cold; gods who took from the people, gods who demanded appeasement, gods who never gave to us or asked us to give to one another. This God was different. This God actually cared about the people.

One day I found myself praying to this God, praying that this God would be kind to Pilate, who understands so little about other people. I told Joseph in confidence about my prayer. Joseph said I had been claimed by God. Joseph called me a child of God . . . I don't know. There's much I don't understand, but somehow I do believe that this God of the Jews does care about me.

Then one day I heard Pilate talking excitedly to one of his soldiers about a man named Jesus. I asked about him. Pilate said he was just some religious fanatic. He said he hoped he wasn't another John the Baptist who would scream in the wilderness.

I asked Joseph about Jesus. At first Joseph looked alarmed, then he looked around as if he were looking to see if anyone was watching us. Then the strangest look came over Joseph's face, and all he said was, "You have to see for yourself, Claudia. He'll be coming into Jerusalem following Sabbath."

You have to see for yourself, Claudia . . . but then Pilate said, "Stay in your quarters, Claudia. . . ." Stay in my quarters? Not likely . . . not likely at all!

And so I went out, wearing my servant's hooded cloak. I stood along the route that Jesus was to travel. The people were holding palm branches. A woman offered one to me, but I shook my head. As Jesus approached, the crowd began yelling and jumping and running. They cried "Hosanna! Hosanna!" They ran along beside him with shouts of welcome . . .

As he passed near me, I stepped back, but was still caught up in the crowd. They jostled and pushed me until I found myself very near to this Jesus of Nazareth. He paused . . . then turned and looked into my eyes and said one word: "Daughter!"

I swayed, dizzy from the look, dizzy from those eyes that seemed to read my soul. I found myself stooping to pick up a palm branch. I stepped toward him, and I, granddaughter of Caesar Augustus, answered, "Raboni!"

And then he was gone, swallowed up by the crowd, the crowd who cheered him on—the same crowd who, this very moment, I can hear screaming through the thickness of these palace walls: "Crucify him! Crucify him!"

Last night Pilate and I sat in the small chamber talking

124

about Jesus and the events of the week. Jesus had been seen pushing over the tables of the moneychangers in the Temple. He had been seen cursing a fig tree. He had been heard outwitting the Sanhedrin as they tried to trap him into blasphemy. Pilate said he feared a riot. Perhaps, he said, Jesus might be assassinated.

"Oh, no!" I cried.

Pilate looked at me and laughed. "Oh, Claudia, do you fear for your Jew? You would do better fearing for your husband, who is trapped between the Jews and Rome! If you want to worry, worry about me instead of one Jew!"

I was about to answer him, about to try and reason with him, about to tell him about my encounter with Jesus, about to tell him what Joseph had told me. I knew Pilate would have listened—but I needed time to tell him carefully, and time I did not have, for we were interrupted by a servant announcing Caiaphas.

I excused myself after getting Pilate to promise to come to my quarters and tell me what Caiaphas wanted at this late hour. It seemed forever before Pilate came to tell me. I've never seen him quite so worried, so anxious, so trapped. "Pilate," I asked, "why do the Jews want to harm Jesus?"

Pilate looked out of the window and said in a tired voice, "It seems this man Jesus has some power over the most powerful of the Jews."

That's what it was all about: Power! The power of Rome . . . the power of Pilate . . . the power of the Sanhedrin . . . the power of Jesus . . . the power of his God. I went to sleep last night thinking of those eyes burning into mine: "Daughter!"

And then the dream . . . the nightmare . . . Pilate, screaming at the crowd: Take him then . . . crucify him if you want to, but don't blame me for it! And I heard the pounding of the nails . . . flesh into wood as the cross was raised . . . and the groaning from the cross, and from beneath the cross—men and women wailing—and then somehow, I, too, was at the foot of the cross, crying, trembling, and through the wailing, I heard him call to me: "Daughter!"

I cried to Pilate to save him, but Pilate didn't hear me because Tiberius was thundering his displeasure, screaming at Pilate that he must leave Judea . . .

And I awoke—and now Pilate's gone.

I must warn Pilate. He doesn't know what's going on . . . a note on this wax tablet . . . a note of warning!

"Have nothing to do with that just man, for I have suffered many things this day in a dream because of him" (Matt. 27:19, KJV).

Pilate! Jesus—is he? What do you mean, they've taken him! What do you mean, you did what you could! How can you wash your hands of the whole affair!

Oh, Pilate, if you're not responsible, who is? If not you, who?

(Claudia moves down the aisle or among the people, looking into their eyes as she repeats three times:)

If not you, who?
If not you, who?
If not you, who?

Then she goes swiftly to the back, crying:
Raboni! Raboni!

SOJOURNER TRUTH,
THE SPIRIT OF CHANGE

Sojourner?
Whoever would name anybody "Sojourner"?
I guess nobody would . . . except maybe God,
and that's what she said: *God gave me my name:*
Sojourner Truth.

1797 . . . in the muddy cellar of an inn,
    she was born . . . black, female, and a slave—
    and yet in 1987 the face of Sojourner Truth
    was on a United States postage stamp.

Bomefree was her father's name;
    Bomefree, meaning "straight as a tree":
    Bomefree carried by slave ship
    from the Gold Coast to New Amsterdam.

Her mother was Mau-mau Bett,
    and she gave birth to a baby girl
    sometime in 1797.
No one bothered to record the exact date . . .

Her name was Isabella Ardinburgh.
    Her master's name was hers.
    Beneath the stars, Mau-mau Bett
    told her children
    about life and about God,
    life on the auction block
    where Mau-mau Bett was to see

her ten children sold away from her.
Mau-mau Bett told her children:
"There is a God who hears and sees you
. . . When you are beaten or cruelly treated,
or fall into any kind of trouble, you must ask help of
   him,
and he will always hear and help you."
When she was nine, Isabella was on the auction block;
   she sold for $100.

Her name was Isabella Nealy.
   She now lived in Ulster County, New York.
   Black, female, slave,
      she spoke only in Dutch jargon,
      infuriating her owners.
   Sunday morning: *Go to the barn, Isabella.*
      Beaten and bleeding, she emerged,
      scarred for life by a white man
      because this little black girl
      couldn't speak English.

But that little ten-year-old girl
   could speak the language of God:
   Protect me, God.
   Deliver me from my persecutors.
Soon after, Nealy sold her.
   This time she brought $105.

Her name was Isabella Scriver.
   She lived in Kingston, New York,
   slave to Martin Scriver,
   fisherman and tavern owner.
Isabella grew strong,
   unloading boats at the wharf,
   working in the tavern.
   Thirteen years old . . . no longer frail and frightened,
   but tall and strong and proud,
   she was sold to a neighbor for $300.

Her name was Isabella Dumont.
   Dumont said she was better than a man,
   for she could do the work of his best hands in the
      field
   and the family's laundry at night.
   He called her "Belle,"
   and she soon became his favorite slave;
   envied by the other slaves,
   disliked by Mrs. Dumont.

It was here Isabella fell in love
   with a slave named Robert
   who lived on the Catlin estate.
   Discovered visiting Isabella,
   Robert was severely beaten
   and forced to marry a Catlin slave
   so that the children would not belong to Dumont.
   Isabella had to marry a Dumont slave.

Isabella had a talk with God.
   It used to be that she thought God had created her a
      slave,
   and so she tried to be the best slave she knew how,
   to be obedient to God.
   Now she realized it was society, not God,
   who made her a slave.
   Her masters could make her decisions:
   they could force her to marry;
   they could sell her children away.
In her conversations with God, God told her
   to work against this evil system.
Oh, Isabella . . . how demeaning . . .
   forced to marry, forced to breed, just like
      the animals . . .
   so the masters can make more money, selling children.

Although Isabella's parents had been freed,
   they had no place to go;

had nothing for their years of slavery.
One evening Bomefree found Mau-mau Bett dead
in the same damp and muddy cellar
where Isabella had been born.
Bomefree, old and blind and grieving,
turned out of his cellar home,
was forced to wander about.
On a winter morning a few years later,
he was found frozen to death.

Every day Isabella went to pray
in her sanctuary among the willow trees.
She began with the Lord's Prayer . . . in Dutch . . .
just as Mau-mau Bett had taught her;
and then she carried on her conversations with God,
questioning, bargaining, praising, pleading.

She longed for July 4, 1827,
when all the slaves in New York State would be set
free.
Dumont even promised to set her free earlier
since she had been such a faithful slave.
When he reneged on his promise,
it was more than Isabella could take.

She had a talk with God:

"Oh, God, I been a-askin' ye an' askin' ye to make my
massa and missis better, an' you don't do it; an' what can
be the reason? . . . Well, now, I tell you, I'll make a bargain
with you. Ef you'll help me to git away from my massa and
missis, I'll agree to be good; but ef you don't help me, I really
don't think I can be."

Escape . . . she couldn't see well enough to escape in the
dark,
but she thought she'd get caught in the daylight.
What'll I do, God?

130

God said: "Git up two or three hours afore daylight,
　　an' start off."
Thank you, Lord . . . "That's a good thought."
Escape . . . 3 A.M. . . . with baby Sophia . . .
　　walk away . . .

Her name was Isabella Van Wagener.
　　Even though Dumont had caught up with her,
　　even though the Van Wageners of the Quaker faith
　　didn't believe in buying human beings but still
　　paid Dumont for the services of Isabella
　　and Sophia for the rest of the year,
　　she was almost free. . . .

Life with the Van Wageners was stifling
　　to the spirited Isabella.
　　When Dumont visited a few months later,
　　she was tempted to return with him,
　　but the Spirit of God came upon Isabella,
　　and nothing was the same anymore.

　　In her *Narrative*, Isabella explains:
　　"Well, jest as I was goin' out to get into the wagon, I
met God! an' says I, 'O God, I didn't know as you was so
great!' An' I turned right around an' come into the house,
an' set down in my room; for 'twas God all around me. I
could feel it burnin', burnin', burnin' all around me, an'
going through me; an' I saw I was so wicked, it seemed as
ef it would burn me up. An' I said, 'Oh, somebody, somebody, stand between God an' me! For it burns me!'
　　"Then . . . I felt as [if] it were somethin' like an amberill
[umbrella] that came between me an' the light, an' I felt it
was somebody . . . I begun to feel 'twas somebody that loved
me . . . an' finally somethin' spoke out in me an' said, 'This
is Jesus.' . . . An' I begun to feel sech a love in my soul as
I never felt before . . . love to all creatures. An' then, all of
a sudden, it stopped, an' I said, 'Dar's de white folks that
have abused you, an' beat you, an' abused your people—

think of them!' But then there came another rush of love
through my soul, an' I cried out loud—'Lord, Lord, I can
love even de white folks!' "

The spirit of God
    burning in Isabella
with a love so powerful that
    she could love those who persecuted her.
The spirit of God
    burning in Isabella so strongly that
    she was not to be stopped.
The spirit of God
    changed what seemed impossible to change.
The spirit of change . . .

Isabella, barefoot, went to the New York Grand Jury in
        Kingston
    to complain that her five-year-old son, Peter,
    had been illegally sold.
    Miraculously, the white slave-owner was arrested
    and made to post $600 in court costs.
    In 1828 a black free woman
    took a white man to court and won:
    Isabella's first landmark case.

In 1829, Isabella moved to New York City,
    joined the Zion African Church,
    and began to work at the Magdalene House.
    When a man named Elijah Pierson died,
    Isabella was accused of poisoning him.
    She sued for slander, and, in another landmark case,
    the all-white male jury acquitted her
    and awarded her $125 in damages!

Isabella decided to set out across the country
    with her message about Jesus.
    Every time she had been sold,
    she had been renamed for her master.
    As she set out on this new venture,

she wanted a new name.
As she walked, the name Sojourner came to her
because she would "travel up and down the land,"
and be "a sign to the people."
What about her last name?
She had a talk with God.
God gave her "Truth," because she was to declare
the truth to the people.
"Thou art my last master, and thy name is Truth; and
  Truth
shall be my abiding name till I die."

And so it began.
With the spirit of God burning within her,
Sojourner Truth set out across the land,
preaching freedom, testifying to God's truth.

And how she could preach!
She spoke fire, but she spoke with compassion,
and the fire of her words ignited the hearts
of the crowd who heard her.
She could not read,
and yet the educated listened to her,
as did the religious and political leaders
of the day.
She had friends among the mighty,
and carried with her the "Book of Life"
signed by people like Harriet Beecher Stowe,
Frederick Douglass, Ulysses Grant, and Abraham
  Lincoln.

Sometimes her presence brought scorn and ridicule
but Sojourner faced the scoffers with dignity,
knowing that the spirit of God was with her.
When Sojourner was told that opponents had threatened
to burn down a meeting hall
where she was to speak in Indiana,
Sojourner replied: "Then I will speak upon the ashes."

At another meeting in Indiana, a local physician accused
Sojourner of being a man because she was six feet tall
and had a low voice.
The doctor called for a vote and
Sojourner was overwhelmingly voted a male.
She stood and spoke:

"I dar'st show my breasts to the whole cong'agation. It
ain't to my shame that I do this, but to yourn. Here den,
see for yourself!" she shouted, and opened her dress from
collar to waist.
Her accusers fled.

There was a terrible thunderstorm during a meeting
where the abolitionist Parker Pillsbury was speaking.
A pro-slavery Methodist minister stood to speak:
"I am alarmed. I feel as if God's judgment is about to
fall upon me for daring to sit and hear such
blasphemy."
Over the loud noise of the thunder,
Sojourner's low voice came loud and clear:
"Chile, don't be skeered; you are not going to be
harmed. I don't 'spec God's ever hearn tell on ye."

At an 1852 women's rights convention in Akron, Ohio,
Sojourner marched to the front of the church
and sat on the pulpit steps.
Her presence brought scorn from the men,
many of them clergy, who had come to argue
against the issue.
Even the women were upset, for they didn't
want their issue weakened by association
with the question of abolition.
On the second day of the convention,
one man asked: "Why should not men have superior
rights and privileges? Just look at their superior
intellects."
Another spoke of Jesus: "If God had desired the equality

of women, he would have given some token of his
will through the birth, life, and death of the Savior."
A third preacher said: "Look at what happened on
account of Eve."

Sojourner had heard enough.
She rose and made her way to the platform.
She could hear the voices saying, "Don't let her speak."
But she did speak:
standing tall in her grey dress with its white collar,
she stooped to lay her bonnet at her feet and
she looked out over the crowd.

"Well, chilern, whar dar is so much racket dar must be
something out o' kilter. I tink dat 'twixt de niggers of de
Souf and de women at de Norf all a-talkin' 'bout rights, de
white men will be in a fix pretty soon. But what's all dis here
talkin' 'bout? Dat man ober dar say dat women needs to be
helped into carriages, and lifted ober ditches, and to have
de best place every whar. Nobody eber help me into carriages, or ober mud puddles, or gives me any best place—"
and, raising herself to her full height and her voice to a pitch
like rolling thunder, she asked, "—and ar'n't I a woman?
Look at me! Look at my arm!" She bared her muscular right
arm to the shoulder. "I have plowed and planted, and gathered into barns, and no man could head me—and ar'n't I
a woman? I could work as much and eat as much as a man
(when I could get it), and bear de lash as well—and ar'n't
I a woman? I have borne thirteen chilern and seen 'em mos'
all sold off into slavery, and when I cried out with a mother's
grief, none but Jesus heard—and ar'n't I a woman? Den dey
talks 'bout dis ting in de head—what dis dey call it?"

"Intellect," whispered someone near.

"Dat's it, honey. What's dat got to do with women's
rights or niggers' rights? If my cup won't hold but a pint and
yourn holds a quart, wouldn't ye be mean not to let me have
my little half-measure full?

"Den dat little man in black dar, he say women can't
have as much rights as man, cause Christ want a woman.

Whar did your Christ come from? Whar did your Christ come from? From God and a woman. Man had nothing to do with him.

"If de fust woman God ever made was strong enough to turn the world upside down, all 'lone, des togedder ought to be able to turn it back and get it right side up again, and now dey is asking to do it, de men better let em. 'Bleeged to ye for hearin' on me, and now old Sojourner ha'nt got nothing more to say."

In the spring of 1864 Sojourner announced
   that she was going down to Washington:
   "I'm going down to advise the President."
   Lincoln said he heard of her before she heard of him.
   He signed in her *Book of Life:*
      For Aunty Sojourner Truth, Oct. 29, 1864, A.
      Lincoln.
Sojourner insisted she had to stay in Washington . . .
   there was so much work to do.
   Sojourner dug in . . . and fought
   hunger and homelessness and illness and
      unemployment . . .
   and discouragement.
   Freedom had been won;
   now Sojourner turned to work for justice.
   She sought a land grant for blacks.
   She took up the causes of temperance
   and child labor. . . .
   She worked for equal pay for equal work. . . .
   This was over a hundred years ago.

In the 1868 election, Sojourner marched
   to the Board of Registration
   to have her name entered on the voting rolls.
On election day she appeared at the polls to vote.
   She was refused.

In 1870 she had an interview with Ulysses Grant
and delivered a petition to Congress concerning land
grants.
She received a standing ovation from the United States
Senate
for her relentless efforts for freedom.

Her age was showing now.
"Everybody tells me to stir 'em up," she said, "but I
ask you, 'Why don't they stir 'em up?' . . . As if a
old body like myself could do all the stirring."

Sojourner returned to visit John Dumont.
Her faith in forgiving him was rewarded, for
he had come to believe that slavery
"is the greatest curse the earth had ever felt."

When she was quite ill, Sojourner said to a friend:
"I'm not going to die, honey.
I'm going home like a shooting star."

What can one person do?
One person can listen to the word of God
and believe in the fire of the spirit of God within her
and set out to tell the truth to the people.
One person can believe that the Holy Spirit
does pour out gifts,
and that these gifts can be used to change
impossible situations.
One person can believe that the Church of Jesus
Christ
has the courage of its convictions;
that together we can burn with a spirit of love
that is so great
we can look the impossible in the face
and say, Change!

SERVICES OF WORSHIP

A SERVICE OF WORSHIP
FOR THE LENTEN SEASON

CALL TO WORSHIP

Six people are needed: minister from pulpit, two adults from each aisle, child in front row.

Minister: When Lent comes you have to put away the tinsel; you have to take down your Christmas tree, and stand out in the open . . . vulnerable.

Second: You either are or you aren't.

Third: You either believe or you don't.

Fourth: You either will or you won't.

Fifth: And, O Lord, how we love the stable and the star!

Minister: When Lent comes the angels' voices begin their lamenting.

Fifth: And we find ourselves in a courtyard where we must answer whether we know him or not.

Second: Lent is a time to take the time to let the power of our faith story take hold of us;

Fourth:	A time to let the events get up and walk around in us;
Third:	A time to intensify our living unto Christ;
Second:	A time to hover over the thoughts of our hearts;
Third:	A time to place our feet in the streets of Jerusalem or to walk along the sea and listen to his word;
Fourth:	A time to touch his robe and feel the healing surge through us;
Fifth:	A time to ponder and a time to wonder . . .
Minister:	Lent is a time to allow a fresh new taste of God!
Child:	*(stands and speaks in a loud voice)* We are one family in the Lord. Let us together worship God.

HYMN OF PRAISE

Suggested: "Sing Praise to God, Who Reigns Above"
Johann J. Schütz, 1675   MIT FREUDEN ZART

PRAYER OF CONFESSION

God of the Covenant, forgive our turning away. Forgive us
for putting you on hold during the week while we busily
live our lives without you. Forgive us for trying to make
you a Sunday God instead of the God of our Lives.
We confess that even though we don't have time for you,
we have time for more work and more recreation and

more projects for our homes. We confess that when we have a problem, we call out your name, but we expect an instant, magical solution. We confess we make little effort to live our faith daily. We confess the arrogance of attempting to feed your sheep when we do not turn to you for nourishment. Help us, Holy One, to remember that we need your bread before we can feed the hungry and your living water before we can offer a cup of cold water in your name.

Please, God of the Covenant, forgive our turning away and have mercy upon us in our returning. We pray in the name of Jesus who is forgiveness and promise. Amen.

THE ASSURANCE OF GOD'S GRACE

RESPONSE TO GOD'S FORGIVING LOVE

V. 3, "Praise the Lord, God's Glories Show"   LLANFAIR
Henry Francis Lyte   Robert Williams

Praise the Lord, great mercies trace, Alleluia!
Praise this providence and grace, Alleluia!
All that God for us has done, Alleluia!
All God sends us through the Son! Alleluia!

ANTHEM

CONCERNS OF THE CHURCH

Welcome, expression of friendship, announcements.

CHILDREN'S SERMON, if one is planned

OLD TESTAMENT READING: Isaiah 58:3–9

Leader:
> Behold, in the day of your fast
> you seek your own pleasure.
> Is such the fast that I choose,

a day for one to humble oneself?
Is it to bow down one's head like a rush,
and to spread sackcloth and ashes?

People:

Is this not rather the fast that I choose:
to let the oppressed go free
and to break every yoke?
Is it not to share your bread with the hungry;
when you see the naked, to cover them?
Then shall your light break forth like the dawn.

Leader:

Then shall you call, and the LORD
will answer;
you shall cry, and the LORD will say,
Here I am.

THE OFFERING

Anthem

DOXOLOGY AND PRAYER OF DEDICATION

NEW TESTAMENT READING Luke 4:16–22 (TEV, adapted)

Leader:

Then Jesus went up to Nazareth, where he had been
brought up, and on the Sabbath he went as usual
to the synagogue. He stood up to read the Scriptures and was handed the book of the prophet
Isaiah. He unrolled the scroll and found the place
where it is written:

People:

"The Spirit of the Lord is upon me,
because he has chosen me
to bring good news to the poor.
He has sent me to proclaim

144

liberty to the captives
and recovery of sight to the blind,
to set free the oppressed
and announce that the time has come
when the Lord will save his people."

Leader:

> Jesus rolled up the scroll, gave it back to the attendant, and sat down. All the people in the synagogue had their eyes on him as he said to them: "This passage of scripture has come true today, as you heard it being read."

People:

> They were all well impressed with him and marveled at the eloquent words that he spoke. They said: "Isn't he the son of Joseph?"

Sermon: Return to Me

(The following script would not, of course, be in the order of worship. Some churches would list the participants here, or they might be listed on the back sheet. Please feel free to adapt as you wish.)

Minister:

> Jesus makes a very good impression in his home town. He has read the scriptures eloquently and all the people in the synagogue marvel at him—*until* he interprets the scriptures. He explained that there were many widows living in Israel during the time of Elijah, and yet Elijah was sent to a widow who was a foreigner. It was the same with Elisha. In his day there were many people with leprosy, and yet only Naaman, the Syrian, was healed. Where does this leave the true believers such as those gathered for worship, listening to Jesus read the scriptures? Verse 28 reads: "When the people in the synagogue heard this, they were filled with anger."

Imagine a Sunday morning in this congregation. Imagine an outside speaker coming in and telling you, who are good church members, that God wants you to take care of people who are not good church people. How would you feel? Would you have the same reaction as the elder brother in the story of the prodigal son? This "outside speaker" is saying that God wants to throw a party for those who don't deserve it, when you've been faithful all along! God wants to throw a party for those who have not been coming to church, when you've been coming to church all the time! Not only that, God wants you to be happy about it and to kill the fatted calf; that is, God wants you to pay for this party, and to rejoice that these undeserving persons have come to church. Angry congregation? Imagine!

First Reader:

We were pleased, Jesus.
You read Isaiah's poem quite well.
We were impressed;
    in fact, we marveled.
We so enjoy hearing familiar passages
    concerning our salvation.
We were pleased, Jesus, until you told your
    stories . . .
    as though God would ignore the true believers
    and pay attention to those who don't deserve it.
It was then we understood
    that the poor and captive
        and oppressed
        of whom you spoke
    were those who had no money, no freedom, no
    power.
We are not pleased, Jesus,
    for we have worked long and hard at
        righteousness

146

And expect to have exclusive rights
  when it comes to salvation.
The Expected One is not the one we expected.*

Lent is traditionally a time of reflection, a time of repentance, a time of renewal. Now, we don't have trouble with reflection. During Lent most of us attend more church services, and some of us read our Bibles and devotional material with greater regularity. And we have great hopes for improvement, for recommitment, for renewal. On Easter Sunday almost everybody comes to worship! But we don't like to think about repentance. The Greek word for repentance, *metanoia*, literally means to turn back toward, to make a U-turn on the road you're traveling. Repentance means to turn back to God.

When we think of Lent and of repentance, we usually think of fasting. What does our Old Testament scripture say about fasting? *Behold, in the day of your fast, you seek your own pleasure.*

Minister:

Wait just one minute! It's certainly no fun to fast! Does God think we're having a good time fasting? Doesn't God appreciate our sacrifice?

Second Reader:

If we do without meat or without desserts or without (heaven forbid!) chocolate for the entire Lenten season, doesn't God know we're making a real effort at repentance?

Minister:

If the people go to all the effort to attend worship and study during Lent, and if they perhaps put a little

---

*From "Advent Calendar," 1987, by Ann Weems, in *Presbyterian Survey.*

more in the offering plate, and if some take on the
discipline of fasting, won't God be pleased with
our righteousness?

First Reader:

Listen to the Prophet Amos.

Amos:

*(coming from the back, speaking as he walks, maybe
stopping from time to time and looking at the people)*
The Lord says: "I hate your religious festivals; I
cannot stand them! When you bring me burnt
offerings and grain offerings, I will not accept
them; I will not accept the animals you have fat-
tened to bring me as offerings. Stop your noisy
songs; I do not want to listen to your harps. Instead, let justice flow down like a stream, and righteousness like a river that never goes dry"
[5:21–24].

First Reader:

"Noisy songs?" Personally, I thought the choir was
quite good.

Amos:

Thus says the Lord: "You like to compose songs, as
David did, and play them on harps . . . but you do
not mourn over the ruin all about you. . . . You do
not come back to me!" [6:5, 6; 4:8]

Minister:

But what about our offerings? During Lent, if people
want to bring extra offerings, isn't that a righteous
thing to do? Won't God be pleased?

Amos:

Thus says the Lord: "Go ahead, bring your offerings every morning! Bring your tithes every third day! Go on and brag about the extra offerings you bring! This is the kind of thing you love to do. And still you do not come back to me." [4:4, 5, 8]

Second Reader:

Somehow I don't even think I should ask about fasting!

Amos:

Thus says the Lord: "Keeping quiet in such evil times is the smart thing to do! . . . You have oppressed the poor and robbed them of their grain! You persecute good people, take bribes, and prevent the poor from getting justice in the courts! . . . You say to yourselves, 'We can hardly wait for the holy days to be over so that we can sell our grain. When will the Sabbath end so we can start selling again?' " [5:11-13; 8:5]

As for fasting . . . you just read what Isaiah said: The fast that God chooses is to let the oppressed go free and break every yoke, to share your bread with the hungry and to cover the naked. [*Speaking tenderly:*] Then shall your light break forth like the dawn. Then shall you call and the LORD will answer; you shall cry, and the LORD will say, Here I am.

Then Amos starts back up the aisle in silence, but as he walks along, perhaps three or four times he turns and says pleadingly, looking directly into the eyes of some of the congregants:

"Come back to the Lord, and live."

149

First Reader:

"Come back to the Lord, and live." . . . Lent is a time for reflection, for repentance, for renewal; a time to turn around, a time to turn back to God, a time to confess our religiosity, and to remember what true worship is. Listen to this parable:

Minister:

Luke 18:9–14, the parable of the Pharisee and the Tax Collector.

(The Minister reads parable as it is written while the story is acted out by two people, the Pharisee *and the* Tax Collector. *The* Pharisee *is dressed very elegantly (you decide whether you want to have him dressed in period costume or modern dress). He strides in proudly, with "pomp and circumstance." The* Tax Collector *is dressed so you'd never notice him in a crowd. He enters almost furtively, not wanting to be seen. . . . The* Pharisee *and the* Tax Collector *act out the story, speaking only when the parable says they prayed.)*

First Reader:

Lent is a time to give our hearts once more, a time to remember our covenant and to give thanks for the new covenant in Jesus Christ. Lent is a time to remember that it was the self-righteous "good church people" that Jesus admonished.

Three readers are needed. They should stand in the front of the sanctuary.

1:	Good church people: Not sinners, they;
2 and 3:	No-o-o-o!
1:	Not lawbreakers;
2 and 3:	No-o-o-o!

150

1:          Not thieves;

2 and 3:   No-o-o-o!

1:          Not adulterers;

2 and 3:   No-o-o-o!

1:          But rulemakers,
            Upstanding,
            Righteous,
            Remarkably wonderful church members.

3:          These good church people asked for a Savior—
            And when he came,
            They knew there had been some mistake.

2:          As long as there were palms to wave
            And alleluias to be sung,

3:          As long as there were stories told
            and promises of good things to come,

1:          As long as there were loaves and fishes
            And rumors of miracles,

3:          The people danced around him and called him
                Rabbi.

1:          But when he lived a little too abundantly for
                their taste
            —for good taste,

2:          When he chose his friends from among ruffians,

1:          Women of the streets,

3:          Tax collectors,

2:      Cursing fishermen,

1:      And then publicly called God his father,
        They knew this wasn't their man.
        So they called him:

3:      Blasphemer,

2:      Lawbreaker,

3:      Sinner-lover.

1:      And they killed him.

*After a pause, have a soloist sing the first verse of the spiritual
    "Were You There When They Crucified My Lord?"*

2:      But that was a long time ago.

3:      Hail, hail, the gang's still here.

1:      Today we are the crowd, screaming:
            He's an agitator.
            He's a revolutionary.
            He tells them to love God,
            Yet he breaks the Sabbath laws.
            He tells them to do good,
            Yet he dines with sinners.
            He tells them to love one another
            Even when they are wronged.
            He tells them to forgive
            Even when no pardon is asked.

2:      Today we are Pilates—
            Unable to make a decision,
            Unable to take a stand,
            Unable to risk our pitiful positions,
            Wringing our hands and saying we're
                not responsible.

3:         Today we are Sadducees and Pharisees—
                Saying we know how to run this temple, thank you!
                Clinging to our written rules,
                Chief among these being:
                    Do not fraternize with the enemy; and
                    Righteous ritual will get you into heaven.

1:         Who do you say God is, by the way you live?

RESPONSE OF THE PEOPLE

(Suggested: "Turn to Me," by John Foley, S.J.; based on Isaiah 45:22, 23; 51:12, 4, 6. Available through North American Liturgy Resources, Phoenix, Arizona, 85029.)

LITANY OF REPENTANCE

Minister:
        How quickly the people changed from "Hosanna!" to "Crucify him!"

People:
        From following to turning away

Minister:
        From listening to turning away

People:
        From seeing to turning away

Minister:
        From covenanting to turning away

People:
        How quickly we change from covenanting to turning away
           From seeing to turning away
           From listening to turning away
           From following to turning away

Minister:
> How quickly we change from "Hosanna!" to "Crucify him!"

People:
> Lord, have mercy upon us!

Minister:
> How easily we promise to live daily in covenant with God!

People:
> Promising to live each day with the intention of being just to others . . .

Minister:
> Christ, have mercy upon us!

People:
> Promising to treat others with compassion . . . each day . . .

Minister:
> Lord, have mercy upon us!

People:
> Promising to be humble . . . each day . . .

All:
> Father, forgive . . .

Minister:
> How grace-filled is our God,
> whose only begotten Son
> fulfilled our part of the covenant

People:
And died that we might live

Minister:
Each day . . . each day . . .

People:
O Lamb of God, have mercy upon us

Minister:
And grant us thy peace.

People:
How grace-filled is our God!

Minister:
Lent is a time to remember that God forgets.

People:
When we turn again, God forgives
and forgets . . .

Minister:
Lent is a time to turn again to God,

People:
To see, to hear, to follow, to covenant,
To live justly, compassionately, humbly;
Lent is a time to come back to the Lord and live.

Minister:
Then shall your light break forth like the dawn.
Then shall you call and the Lord will answer;

People:
We shall cry, and the Lord will say, Here I am.

HYMN   Suggested: "O God, our Faithful God"

Johann Heermann, 1630   O GOTT, DU FROMMER GOTT

BENEDICTION *(said by a child)*

The Lord bless you and keep you while we are absent one
from the other.

A SERVICE OF WORSHIP FOR PENTECOST: THE SEVEN GIFTS OF THE SPIRIT

In preparation for worship, read in the pew Bible Genesis 1:1–2; Acts 2:1–21.

PRELUDE

INTROIT

CALL TO WORSHIP

Minister: Why is this day different from all the other days of the week?

People: This is the Lord's Day; let us be glad and rejoice in this day, set apart for rest and remembering and thanks-giving!

Minister: All blessing and honor and glory and power and riches and wisdom and strength be to the Lamb who was slain! Let us worship God!

HYMN IN PROCESSION

"O for a Thousand Tongues to Sing"   AZMON

In life and in death we belong to God.
   Through the grace of our Lord Jesus Christ,
      the love of God,
         and the communion of the Holy Spirit,
   we trust in the one triune God, the Holy One of
   Israel,
      whom alone we worship and serve.

. . . .

We trust in God the Holy Spirit,
      everywhere the giver and renewer of life.
   The Spirit justifies us by grace through faith,
      sets us free to accept ourselves and to love God and
      neighbor,
      and binds us together with all believers
      in the one body of Christ, the church.
   The same Spirit
      who inspired the prophets and apostles
      rules our faith and life in Christ through Scripture,
      engages us through the Word proclaimed,
      claims us in the waters of baptism,
      feeds us with the bread of life and the cup of
      salvation,
      and calls women and men to all ministries of the
      Church.
   In a broken and fearful world
   the Spirit gives us courage
      to pray without ceasing,
      to witness among all peoples to Christ as Lord and
      Savior,
      to unmask idolatries in church and culture,
      to hear the voices of peoples long silenced,
      and to work with others for justice, freedom, and
      peace.
   In gratitude to God, empowered by the Spirit,

we strive to serve Christ in our daily tasks
   and to live holy and joyful lives,
even as we watch for God's new heaven and new
   earth,
     praying, Come, Lord Jesus!

With believers in every time and place,
   we rejoice that nothing in life or in death
   can separate us from the love of God in Christ Jesus
   our Lord.

Glory be to the Father, and to the Son, and to the Holy
   Spirit. Amen.*

THE DOXOLOGY

ANTHEM

EXPRESSION OF FRIENDSHIP

OFFERING

"O for the Wings of a Dove" (Hear My Prayer)
F. Mendelssohn

PRAYER OF DEDICATION

OFFERTORY RESPONSE

"Come, Thou Fount of Every Blessing"   NETTLETON

   Come, Thou Fount of every blessing,
   Tune my heart to sing thy grace;
   Streams of mercy, never ceasing,
   Call for songs of loudest praise.
   Teach me some melodious sonnet,
   Sung by flaming tongues above;

---

*From "A Brief Statement of Faith: Presbyterian Church (U.S.A.)," in
*The Minutes of the General Assembly of the Presbyterian Church
(U.S.A.),* Part I: Journal, p. 268.

Praise the mount! I'm fixed upon it,
Mount of God's unchanging love.

THE READING OF THE SCRIPTURE: Ezekiel 37:1–6;
Revelation 5

The Seven Gifts of the Spirit

(The congregation has a part in this portion of the service of worship. We ask that you turn to the front page of the bulletin insert at this point.)

The Bringing Forth of the Elements

Invitation to the Lord's Table

Communion Hymn: "The Lone, Wild Bird"
Richard Henry McFadyen, 1925   PROSPECT

Distribution of the Elements

(Elders will assist you in moving to the tables for communion.)

Response of Faith

Bless our time together here, O God, and may our renewal be so visible to those we meet that your name will be praised. In the name of the Lamb who was slain, we pray. Amen.

Benediction Response: "Worthy Is the Lamb"
Revelation 5:12   Handel's *Messiah*

Postlude

Notes for "The Seven Gifts of the Spirit"

In chancel area, mounted vertically so it faces the congregation, is a "wheel" with seven doves facing inward and the names of seven gifts of the Spirit written between the doves. As individuals speak of each gift, they put their hand on the dove next to the gift, and move the wheel so that the gift being considered is at the top of the wheel.

Also in the chancel will be seven wrapped gifts, containing the following:

1) The largest (we used a wardrobe box from a moving company) contains fifty red helium balloons with their strings attached to a heavy object so that when the lid of the box is removed, the "bouquet" of balloons springs up and out of the box but the strings remain in the box. This largest box will also contain long red cloth or crepe paper "streamers." For our sanctuary, which has a middle aisle, we had four people, two in the middle aisle and one on each side aisle, carry two streamers each over the heads of the seated congregation. The red streamers represent the Spirit traveling over the people.
2) A birthday cake, which the congregation can eat after the service.
3) The Bible.
4) A sign with white raised symbols on it (in red, it reads JESUS).
5) A framed copy of Philippians 4:13.

6) A red balloon with a white dove on it (order enough of these for everyone in the congregation to have one).
7) A red balloon with a white heart on it. Write LOVE OF GOD on the white heart.

Also in the chancel area is a pile of bones, prominently placed in the center.

One person will serve as the Interpreter, and seven persons will be the Believers.

Script for "The Seven Gifts of the Spirit"

(The Interpreter walks to pulpit from congregation. The Believers also rise from the congregation and move forward to examine the chancel area. Several Children should be ready to sing the first verse and chorus of "Jesus Loves Me, This I Know" at the proper time.)

First Believer:

> What is all this? I thought we were going to have a birthday party for the Church! Where is the birthday cake? Where are the streamers? Where are the balloons?

Second Believer:

> All this talk of the sealed scroll and creatures around the throne and bones! I don't understand any of it! What does the Spirit say to us in the Church today?

Third Believer:

> Well, the Spirit does give gifts to us . . . and, as luck would have it, here are some gifts!

Fourth Believer:

> *(reading from the wheel)* Blessing and honor and glory and power and riches and wisdom and

strength. Seven gifts of the Spirit . . . what does all that mean?

Fifth Believer:
Well, Pentecost is the time when the Church began, the time when the Holy Spirit came to Jesus' followers.

Sixth Believer:
And the Church is given gifts of the Spirit.

Seventh Believer:
Guess this is it, then . . .

First Believer:
(with hand on wheel, but since blessing *will be at the top, without moving wheel)* Blessing . . . will the Spirit bring us success and prosperity?

Second Believer:
(moving wheel so that honor *is at top)* Honor . . . I think it would be wonderful to have other people speak of me with awe: She is a woman of great honor. Would the Spirit give me the gift of *honor?*

Third Believer:
(moving glory *to the top)* Glory. If Honor's good, *glory* would be . . . uh-h-h . . . uh-h-h . . . *glorious!* Would the Spirit give me glory?

Interpreter:
The *blessing* and *honor* and *glory* of which we speak do not belong to us, but to the Creator. This passage from Revelation refers to the magnitude of God's gift: the Crucified and Risen Christ. When we whom God created understand this gift—that God would give the only Son—then we who have

received the Gift kneel and give all blessing and honor and glory to God.

In our Scripture, John sees in the hand of God a scroll which holds the secrets of things to come, but the scroll is sealed, and no one on earth is worthy to open it, nor are any of the angels worthy. John begins to weep; then he is told that there is One who has conquered and is worthy. When John looks, instead of a mighty conqueror, he sees a lamb, standing as though it had been slain in sacrifice, wounded . . . yet not dead, but alive.

And a chorus of living creatures and the elders and angels, numbering myriads and myriads and thousands and thousands, sing praise to the Lamb who was slain. Of the Believers, I ask: Who is worthy of the *blessing?*

Congregation:
Only the Lamb who was slain.

Interpreter:
And who is worthy of the *honor?*

Congregation:
Only the Lamb who was slain.

Interpreter:
And who is worthy of the *glory?*

Congregation:
Only the Lamb who was slain.

Congregation:
(singing; "At the Name of Jesus," Ralph Vaughan Williams, verse 1):
At the name of Jesus, Every knee shall bow,
Every tongue confess Him King of glory now;

'Tis the Father's pleasure We should call Him Lord,
Who from the beginning Was the mighty Word.

Fourth Believer:

Well . . . there's still *power*. Power's something people on earth have. It would be great to be powerful! Of course, if I had power I would use it for good things! I would stop war and poverty and drug dealing and anything else I didn't like. Oh, if I had power, it'd be great!

Interpreter:

The power of God is opposed to any quest for power on the part of an individual or group . . . even to one congregation or one denomination. The power of God that Jesus proclaimed is the power to redeem and to give new life to the powerless in this world.

In the Revelation passage, Jesus is worthy of the gift of *power* because He was willing to be slain in order that the people of God might be saved. In this scripture, not only is God seen as the sovereign Creator, but God is also seen as the Love that takes on all the sins of the world. Of the Believers I ask: Who is worthy of the gift of *power?*

Congregation:

Only the Lamb who was slain.

Fourth Believer:

So, as Christians, we don't receive the gift of power?

Interpreter:

Christians do receive power from the Spirit, but it is not the *power* of the Lamb who was slain. Why don't you open one of the gifts?
(The Fourth Believer pulls from one of the gift boxes

a balloon with a dove and the word SHALOM *on it;
also in the box is this message:)*

Fourth Believer:

"The power that we receive from the Holy Spirit is
the power to witness to our faith, both by our
words and by our living." There's a Scripture here:
Listen, you who have ears to hear: Acts 1:8: "You
shall receive power when the Holy Spirit has come
upon you; and you shall be my witnesses in Jerusalem and in all Judea and Samaria and to the end
of the earth."

Fifth Believer:

Hm-m-m . . . I don't even need to ask. I *know* I don't
get riches . . . do I?

Interpreter:

The Spirit bestows great riches on the faithful, but it
is not the riches of the world. It is not money, nor
is it cars or furs or jewelry. The *riches* of which we
speak are the riches of the Kingdom of God. Jesus
teaches that the real treasure is in trusting in God.
Your greatest treasure is the love of God written upon
your heart. Believers, who is worthy to receive the
gift of *riches?*

Congregation:

Only the Lamb who was slain.

Interpreter:

You, too, may receive your inheritance. Open your
gift.
*(The Fifth Believer opens a gift and pulls out a red
balloon with a white heart on it, on which is written*
THE LOVE OF GOD; *there are also seven small red
stick-on hearts with* THE LOVE OF GOD *written on
each one; and there is a message:)*

168

Fifth Believer:

"Our inheritance is our faith. We are rich in the only thing that matters, and ours is the Kingdom of God." And there's a Scripture: Listen, you who have ears to hear: 2 Cor. 8:9: "You know the grace of our Lord Jesus Christ, that though he was rich, yet for your sakes he became poor, so that by his poverty you might become rich." *(While congregation sings, the Fifth Believer sticks red hearts onto their shirts.)*

Congregation:

(singing; "Be Thou My Vision" [Irish ballad], verse 2):

Riches I heed not, nor vain, empty praise,
Thou mine inheritance, now and always;
Thou and Thou only, first in my heart,
Great God of Heaven, my treasure Thou art.

Sixth Believer:

Well, listen . . . forget it. I know for sure that the Spirit is not going to give me *wisdom!* I mean . . . I've already asked for it, and so far . . .

Interpreter:

Certainly not the wisdom our world values. The *wisdom* of which we speak is rooted in a right attitude toward God. Believers, who among us is worthy to receive the gift of *wisdom?*

Congregation:

Only the Lamb who was slain.

Interpreter (to Sixth Believer):

Why don't you open a gift?
(The Sixth Believer pulls a Bible out of a gift box, with a message:)

169

Sixth Believer:

"The knowledge of God is found within this Book. 'God has made Christ to be our wisdom: First Corinthians 1:24.' " *(Pulls out a red and white sign saying* JESUS *and holds it up to congregation.)* "Those who see Jesus know the Way, the Truth, and the Life: John 14:6."

Congregation:

(singing; "Be Thou My Vision," verse 3):

Be Thou my Wisdom, and Thou my true word,
I ever with Thee and Thou with me, Lord,
Thou my great Father, I thy true [one],
Thou in me dwelling and I with thee one.

Seventh Believer:

Strength . . . well, I know of a lot of very good people who are strong, but I've been listening, and I know that we're not talking about working out or jogging or keeping fit. We're talking about the strength of the Christ who was strong in God no matter what happened to him . . . right?

Interpreter:

Absolutely right! Strong . . . even to the Cross. Even when his disciples deserted him, even when people said all manner of evil against him, he was strong in the Lord. Believers, who is worthy to receive the gift of *strength?*

Congregation:

Only the Lamb who was slain.

Seventh Believer:

What about our gift? Aren't we followers given strength?

Interpreter:

> Open your gift . . .

Seventh Believer:

> "In your weakness you will be made strong." What does that mean?

Interpreter:

> I imagine the children can tell you.

Children:

> (singing; "Jesus Loves Me," William Batchelder Bradbury; verse 1 and chorus.)

Seventh Believer:

> Oh, I understand. When I realize how dependent I am on Christ, I am strong. "I can do all things through Christ who strengthens me"; Philippians 4:15.

Third Believer:

> Uh-h-h, I don't want to seem complaining, but you let those four people open gifts, and you didn't let us open gifts. Are there other gifts of the Spirit for the Church?

Second Believer:

> And will you tell me what those bones are doing there?

First Believer:

> Yeah, and I thought we were going to have a Pentecost party!

Interpreter:

> Let me explain about the bones first. Did you listen to the Scripture reading from Ezekiel?

Second Believer:

> Yes, but we didn't understand it.

Interpreter:
>
> The dry bones represent God's people when they do not keep covenant; when they do not have the love of God written on their hearts but they have idolatry and greed and self-love written on their hearts. The promise is that the Spirit of God will breathe new life into the people and that they will live again. This is the power of renewal that we see in God's world as winter turns into springtime. We don't work all winter so that Spring will come; it is God who breathes life into the earth. So it is with us; when we wither and die like the trees and the flowers, God has the power to change our dry bones into life-giving faithfulness.
>
> These letters to the seven Churches of John's time are found in Revelation. They give us an all-too-familiar picture of church life.

First Believer:
>
> The Church at Ephesus is commended for its hard work and patience, but there is faction and division and a real lack of enthusiasm.

Second Believer:
>
> The Church at Smyrna has financial problems and has suffered from the persecution, but is warned of more persecution to come, and told to remain loyal to Christ and they will receive life everlasting.

Third Believer:
>
> The Church at Pergamum is commended for its faithfulness, but warned that some of the people are compromising their faith and going along with the idolatrous and immoral practices of the state religion.

172

Fourth Believer:

The Church at Thyatira is too tolerant of unwholesome practices.

Fifth Believer:

The Church at Sardis is told to wake up and remember who they are and to turn from their sins.

Sixth Believer:

The Church at Laodicea is told they are neither hot nor cold and Christ wishes they were one or the other, but is displeased at their lukewarm faith!

Seventh Believer:

The Church at Philadelphia is commended wholeheartedly for being such a loving congregation!

Second Believer:

Only the Church at Philadelphia? Oh, that's frightening! Maybe they had somebody there with a special power of the Spirit!

Interpreter:

Anyone who claims to have special powers of the Spirit is not of God but a false prophet. The Spirit gives power to the Church to help the Church to bring in the Kingdom of God, not to give glory to any one person or group. We aren't gathered here to improve the image of [your church's name] Church. We're not here to seek power for [your church's name] Church; we're not here to seek power for any one of us. Together, we are here to seek the power of the Holy Spirit, that this whole world might know new life through Jesus Christ who taught us to give away our hearts *(participants go out into the congregation and take their heart stickers off and attach them to seven people, smile, and return to chancel area)*:

who taught us a love that praises our Creator
  a love that shares our bread
  a love that includes
who taught us to touch the untouchables
  to accept the unacceptables
  to love the unlovables.

(To **Second Believer:**) If you would have these bones live, come to the table of the One who was broken that we might be made whole. Come to this table and pray that we might together make a difference in this world in the name of Him who said, *Love one another.*

(To **Third Believer:**) Gifts? They are here for the taking.

(To **First Believer:**) Celebration? Yes, indeed, let us celebrate!

(They open their gifts: birthday cake, balloons, and streamers, in that order.)

While the congregation sings "Blessing and Honor," the First Believer *takes the birthday cake down the center aisle or to the back of the church. The* Fourth and Seventh Believers *detach two of the balloons from the bunch and follow the* First Believer *down the aisle. If you have no center aisle, the cake goes down one side, and balloons down the other. Simultaneously, the* Second and Third Believers *drape two of the long red streamers over pews down the center or side aisles and the* Fifth and Sixth Believers *drape streamers over the edge of the communion table. If you can accommodate four tables for communion, the* Second and Third Believers *can instead attach their streamers to a weighted pole, disguised by red cloth, or any high spot, such as the pulpit, and bring the ends over the heads of the members of the congregation and attach the ends to the two tables in the back of the*

174

sanctuary, while the Fifth and Sixth Believers *attach their streamers to the front tables. The* Interpreter *meanwhile has gathered the bones up into a basket that was under the front pew and has put a butterfly, a symbol of new life, in their place. We used a beautiful, large butterfly encased in Plexiglas because we happened to have it, but a large, colorful butterfly can easily be made and placed so it looks as though it might take flight. The* Interpreter *and the* Fifth and Sixth Believers *exit down the center aisle, and the* Ministers *invite the congregation to celebrate communion.*

Congregational Participation, "The Seven Gifts of the Spirit"

The following will need to be included with the order of worship. It may be easiest to put it on an insert sheet.

[Name of designated Interpreter] will give you a cue.

Blessing, Honor, and Glory

Interpreter:
Of the Believers, I ask: Who is worthy of the *blessing?*

Congregation:
Only the Lamb who was slain.

Interpreter:
And who is worthy of the *honor?*

Congregation:
Only the Lamb who was slain.

Interpreter:
And who is worthy of the *glory?*

Congregation:
Only the Lamb who was slain.
(Congregation sings, "At the Name of Jesus," verse 1):

At the name of Jesus, Every knee shall bow,
Every tongue confess Him King of glory now;
'Tis the Father's pleasure We should call Him
    Lord,
Who from the beginning Was the mighty Word.

POWER

Interpreter:
Of the Believers I ask: Who is worthy of the gift of
power?

Congregation:
Only the Lamb who was slain.

RICHES

Interpreter:
Believers, who is worthy to receive the gift of *riches?*

Congregation:
Only the Lamb who was slain.
(After the opening of a gift, Congregation sings, "Be
Thou My Vision," verse 2):

Riches I heed not, nor vain, empty praise,
Thou mine inheritance, now and always;
Thou and Thou only, first in my heart,
Great God of Heaven, my treasure Thou art.

WISDOM

Interpreter:
Believers, who among us is worthy to receive the gift
of *wisdom?*

Congregation:
> Only the Lamb who was slain.
> (After another gift is opened, Congregation sings,
> "Be Thou My Vision," verse 3):

> Be Thou my Wisdom, and Thou my true word;
> I ever with Thee and Thou with me, Lord;
> Thou my great Father, I thy true [one],
> Thou in me dwelling and I with thee one.

STRENGTH

Interpreter:
> Believers, who is worthy to receive the gift of
> *strength?*

Congregation:
> Only the Lamb who was slain.

> (After opening the last gifts, Congregation sings,
> "Blessing and Honor," verse 1):

> Blessing and honor and glory and power,
> Wisdom and riches and strength evermore,
> Give we to Christ who our battle has won,
> Whose are the kingdom, the crown, and the
> throne.

A PROCESSION
TO BETHLEHEM

When our fall adult Christian education class concentrated on biblical characters enacted by the members of our congregation, we knew we needed a "bridge" to Advent and to the New Testament stories that were to be dramatized in the spring. The following piece is the result.

The Old Testament characters processed into the chapel, where we hold our class, and up to the front, and gathered around a Christmas tree just as any family does when it gets together to decorate the tree. Our class was concerned with applying stories from the past to our present-day discipleship. We were about to enter into Advent, and wanted this class to remind us that the Advent story is a story of God's advent today as well as in the year Jesus was born.

All the characters processed in except Eve, who told her story from behind a huge Bible that was made so that each character could step out of its pages into the present. Eve was always hidden, as she hid from God in the garden.

Along with the Bible and the Christmas tree in the front of the chapel were three or four large boxes in which our Christmas ornaments had been stored. We each had chosen an ornament that symbolized our story. One by one, we pulled our ornaments from the boxes and commented on them, recounting memories and telling stories about the ornament, as we hung each ornament on the tree. A poem was read after each biblical character had hung his or her ornament on the tree.

Of course, you do not need to do an adult ed class to use this piece. You also may choose other biblical characters.

A Procession to Bethlehem: Script

A Christmas tree is set up next to the Bible. There will be boxes wrapped in tissue paper, which will hold the ornaments (symbols of the stories). The group will "ooh" and "aah" and generally be excited about unpacking the Christmas decorations. Then one by one each biblical character will "find" the appropriate ornament and hang it on the tree.

Choir: "How Far Is It to Bethlehem?" (English traditional)*

(On last verse, the Biblical Characters *process from the back of the room, with the exception of* Eve, *who remains behind the large Bible.)*

Ruth *hangs an ornament on the tree.*

(We used two readers, who took turns, one standing on each side of the room.)

Reader: How expansive God's love that Ruth
who gleaned in the fields of Boaz
was accepted
chosen
blessed
though she was both widow and foreigner!

**Carols for Choirs, Book 2: Fifty Carols for Christmas and Advent,* ed. and arr. David Willcocks and John Rutter (New York: Oxford University Press, 1970).

How appropriate that Ruth found God in
Bethlehem
where later the whole world found God
when Jesus, who was of her lineage, was born!

Moses *hangs an ornament on the tree.*

Reader: We, like Moses, make our excuses:
"Who are we to go?"
But the God who answered Moses is
the God who answers us:
Certainly I will be with you.
The God who lives in a burning bush
is the God who pitches a tent in our midst
and dwells among us.
Moses said, "Here am I," and took his shoes off.
Let's pray that we, on our way to Bethlehem this
year,
will recognize holy ground when we see it.

Noah *hangs an ornament on the tree.*

Reader: It was faith that made Noah go into the unknown
amid the jeering crowd
against the conventional wisdom.
It was faith that made Noah
prepare for rain that was not predicted
and hold a two-by-two parade into the ark.
It was faith that kept Noah going
through a flood the likes of which
the world has never seen,
the wrath of God raining on the faithless.
Because of faith, Noah collected promises
on dry land
where first of all he and his family
knelt
and gave thanks to God
who made a new promise: Never again!

Daniel *hangs an ornament on the tree.*

Reader: When Daniel wouldn't play politics
and was faithful to God
even though it cost him a promotion,
he was thrown to the lions.
In this time, even we in the church
play politics,
stepping on one another for positions.
Avoiding lions' dens at all costs,
we forget we can pray.
I guess we don't trust God
to send an angel to shut the lions' mouths
even though God sent the Promised One.

David *hangs an ornament on the tree.*

Reader: He was a man after God's own heart,
but a man given to slaying giants and
tens of thousands,
and sending into battle the husband
of the woman he loved.
What is it God saw in David?

David, though he broke covenant,
asked God's forgiveness,
and faithfully returned to covenant living.
He was a man who fought for others,
a man who danced for joy around
the Ark of the Covenant,
a man who believed
and led his people in the ways of God,
a man who loved God inside out
and wanted to show his love
by building a house for God—
but the building was to be left to his son.

So beloved he was by God, however,
that God promised him a house,
the Root and Offspring of David,
the Bright and Morning Star . . .

He who was born in Bethlehem
was of the House of David.

(Eve's arm appears as she taps Moses *on the shoulder.
He turns, but, seeing no one, turns back to the tree. She clears
her throat loudly.* Moses *turns and* Eve's *arm appears again,
and she holds her ornament for* Moses *to hang upon the tree.
He obliges.)*

Reader: It was not the eating of the apple,
     nor listening to the serpent;
   Eve, sister, your sin
     and that of women since,
   is hiding
     from God.
   Content to live on the sidelines,
     afraid to speak up, we listen;
     afraid to lead, we follow;
     afraid to be what God created us to be,
       we hide.
   Perhaps if we come out of the shadows,
     and see ourselves
       in the Light of the Morning Star,
   we might be able to see our way to Bethlehem.

Jonah *hangs an ornament on the tree.*

Reader: It was not really about the whale;
     it was about learning who God really is:
       God, of all people,
       a God of mercy!
         a mercy that includes the Ninevites
           (that's the enemy!)
         and pagan sailors
           (what happened to piety?)
         and even beasts of the field
           (what!?)
   God said it again on a cold night in Bethlehem
     when Christ, surrounded by the beasts,
   was born to save the world.

Sarah *hangs an ornament on the tree.*

Reader: Sarah,
you are not the only one to laugh at God,
nor are you the only one to deny it.
We who claim to be faithful
laugh at God's promises.
Oh, we deny it on Sunday morning,
but go out laughing on Monday.
If we really believed,
we'd be out giving birth
to a world where we all loved each other
even as much as we love ourselves.

Hagar *hangs an ornament on the tree.*

Reader: Even when we feel driven to run
and find we have wandered into the desert,
God sends us water.
Hagar found God in the wilderness
and later gave birth to a son called
Ishmael, "God hears."
We are all Hagars,
wandering in deserts of our own making.
How wondrous to know that God hears
and sends the Living Water.

Job *hangs an ornament on the tree.*

Reader: Job learned what we have yet to learn:
that God's promise was not
to exempt the faithful from pain;
God's promise was to come into our darkness.
The people who walked in darkness
have seen a great light;
those who dwelt in a land of deep darkness,
on them has light shined.

Choir *sings "Star-Light."** On the last verse,* Mary *and*
Joseph, *with the babe, process from the back of the room. The*

---

*"Star-Light," by Ron Ellis. Copyright © 1979 Raven Music. Found in
Glory and Praise, vol. 2, published by North American Liturgy Resources,
Phoenix, Ariz., 85029.

Biblical Characters *pull the manger out in front of the tree and, when* Mary *puts the Child in the manger, they kneel around* Mary *and* Joseph *and the Child.*

Reader: Into this silent night
        as we make our weary way
            we know not where,
    just when the night becomes its darkest,
        and we cannot see our path,
    just then
        is when the angels rush in,
            their hands full of stars.

Reader: We are all part of the procession and heirs of the promise as we walk toward the Star of Bethlehem. You who are descendants of these faithful ones, we invite you to join the procession to Bethlehem—to follow the Star until you find the Christ child. Abraham and Sarah were promised as many descendants as there are stars in the sky . . . and here you are, descendants in faith. As you leave this [morning, evening], we ask you to join the procession to Bethlehem, to come forward and receive from this great cloud of witnesses a sign of the Promise: a star to hold before you as you go into Advent; a star to remind you that we who live in faith are as many as the stars in the sky and that together we will kneel this year in Bethlehem, for unto us a son is born, a savior who is Christ the Lord. He is the Bright and Morning Star.

(Sarah's *ornament was a long wire wrapped with gold with small foil stars attached. It had been purchased, but if you can't find one, you can make your own or just have the* Biblical Characters *hand out stars to each person. The* choir *continues to sing until each person has a star and the* Biblical Characters *have recessed from the room.*)